T0340012

"Marcia Scheiner has done it again with a second resource that will prove to be a value add for companies seeking to employ individuals on the Autism Spectrum, in addition to providing clear and direct examples for individuals that are seeking employment. Ms. Scheiner's overview of how to apply this resource is extremely helpful. Her ability to provide history, application, and foundational principles as a starting point is straightforward and effective. The strategic use of statistics, tables, and flowcharts is helpful as they allow the reader to visualize steps and processes. I see this book being used heavily with a dual focus that benefits employers and potential employees."

– Jamell G. Mitchell, EY NCoE Global
Community Engagement/Ecosystem Leader

"As organizations become increasingly conscious of the imperative of more neurodiversity-inclusive practices, staff in key roles require support and resources to recognize and address potential pitfalls. Marcia Scheiner's latest book – following the successful blueprint of her first – is packed with information and tips while also being neatly structured and highly navigable. The practices she highlights will help individual recruiters and their organizations conduct hiring that is more intentional, more inclusive, and ultimately more successful."

– Ed Thompson, Founder & CEO, Uptimize

"What a wonderfully practical and helpful book for employers on why and how to hire autistic people; and for autistic people on how to improve your chances of getting a job. Clearly written and accessible, Marcia Scheiner makes the case for why all employers should embrace neurodiversity."

– Professor Simon Baron-Cohen, Cambridge University

"Marcia Scheiner's *The Neurodivergent Job Candidate: Recruiting Autistic Professionals* is a book long overdue. As we emerge from a post-COVID world, smart businesses will look to diversify their employment efforts to include neurodivergent people. I know from my prior position as CEO of Specialisterne USA, best intentions and publicized desire to hire neurodiverse people do not reach far enough to make an impact. Current recruitment processes screen out potential neurodivergent applicants, resulting in an erroneous belief that there are not enough neurodiverse candidates with the required skills. *The Neurodivergent Job Candidate* is a must-read to fill in the gaps in common recruitment efforts, allowing companies to screen in this exceptional talent."

– Tara Cunningham, Founder, Beyond-Impact

The Neurodivergent Job Candidate
Recruiting Autistic Professionals

This book provides guidance on recruiting, interviewing, and onboarding practices that will allow employers to successfully hire neurodivergent professionals into inclusive, competitive employment.

Today, 35% of 18-year-olds with an autism spectrum diagnosis attend college, yet they have a 75–85% under-employment and unemployment rate after graduation. While organizations are looking to expand their diversity and inclusion hiring efforts to include neurodivergent professionals, current recruiting and interviewing practices in general are not well-suited to this. With over one-third of the US population identifying as neurodivergent, employers need to address how to attract this talent pool to take advantage of a meaningful segment of the workforce. Readers of this book will gain an understanding of how to guide their organizations through the creation of recruiting, interviewing, and onboarding processes tailored to neurodivergent professionals in any field.

Written by authors with extensive experience working in the corporate world and consulting with Fortune 1000 companies on autism hiring efforts, this book is targeted at employers, acknowledging their perspective. Structured as a reference guide for busy recruiters, hiring managers, and supervisors, this book can be read in its entirety, in relevant sections as needed, or used as a refresher whenever necessary. This book also provides a background on the thinking styles of autistic individuals, giving the reader a deeper understanding of how to best support neurodivergent jobseekers.

Tracy Powell-Rudy is a contributing author of this book.

Marcia Scheiner is the President and Founder of Integrate Autism Employment Advisors (Integrate), co-author of *An Employer's Guide to Managing Professionals on the Autism Spectrum* (2017), and frequent speaker on autism employment. Prior to founding Integrate in 2010, Ms. Scheiner held senior management positions in the financial services industry. Ms. Scheiner is a graduate of Wellesley College, Massachusetts and has an MBA from Columbia University's Graduate School of Business, New York. She is the parent of an adult son with autism.

Joan Bogden is a Content and Media Training Coach and the President of Blonde 'n Blue Productions, as well as the co-author of *An Employer's Guide to Managing Professionals on the Autism Spectrum* (2017). She has over 30 years of experience in the communications and training industry and has a BA in psychology from Vassar College. Ms. Bogden received an MA in clinical psychology from Fordham University, where she was also a published researcher and a doctoral candidate in that field.

The Neurodivergent Job Candidate

Recruiting Autistic Professionals

Marcia Scheiner, Integrate Autism Employment Advisors, and Joan Bogden

Routledge
Taylor & Francis Group

NEW YORK AND LONDON

First published 2022
by Routledge
605 Third Avenue, New York, NY 10158

and by Routledge
2 Park Square, Milton Park, Abingdon, Oxon, OX14 4RN

Routledge is an imprint of the Taylor & Francis Group, an Informa business

© 2022 Marcia Scheiner and Joan Bogden

The rights of Marcia Scheiner and Joan Bogden to be identified as
authors of this work have been asserted by them in accordance with
sections 77 and 78 of the Copyright, Designs and Patents Act 1988.

All rights reserved. No part of this book may be reprinted or
reproduced or utilized in any form or by any electronic, mechanical, or
other means, now known or hereafter invented, including photocopying
and recording, or in any information storage or retrieval system,
without permission in writing from the publishers.

Trademark notice: Product or corporate names may be trademarks
or registered trademarks, and are used only for identification and
explanation without intent to infringe.

Library of Congress Cataloging-in-Publication Data
Names: Scheiner, Marcia, author. | Bogden, Joan, author.
Title: The neurodivergent job candidate: recruiting autistic professionals/
Marcia Scheiner and Joan Bogden.
Description: New York, NY: Routledge, 2022. | Includes bibliographical
references and index.
Subjects: LCSH: Autistic people–Employment. | Autism spectrum
disorders–Patients–Employment.
Classification: LCC HD7255 .S238 2022 (print) | LCC HD7255 (ebook) |
DDC 331.5/95–dc23
LC record available at https://lccn.loc.gov/2021023295
LC ebook record available at https://lccn.loc.gov/2021023296

ISBN: 978-0-367-68389-4 (hbk)
ISBN: 978-0-367-68388-7 (pbk)
ISBN: 978-1-003-13730-6 (ebk)

DOI: 10.4324/9781003137306

Typeset in Sabon
by Deanta Global Publishing Services, Chennai, India

For neurodivergent jobseekers everywhere.

Contents

Authors and Contributors

CO-AUTHORS:

Marcia Scheiner is the President and Founder of Integrate Autism Employment Advisors (Integrate), co-author of *An Employer's Guide to Managing Professionals on the Autism Spectrum* (2017), and frequent speaker on autism employment. Prior to founding Integrate in 2010, Ms. Scheiner held senior management positions in the financial services industry. Ms. Scheiner is a graduate of Wellesley College and has an MBA from Columbia University's Graduate School of Business. She is the parent of an adult son with autism.

Joan Bogden is a Content and Media Training Coach and the President of Blonde 'n Blue Productions, as well as the co-author of *An Employer's Guide to Managing Professionals on the Autism Spectrum* (2017). She has over 30 years of experience in the communications and training industry and has a BA in psychology from Vassar College. Ms. Bogden received an MA in clinical psychology from Fordham University, where she was also a published researcher and a doctoral candidate in that field.

CONTRIBUTOR:

Tracy Powell-Rudy is Integrate Autism Employment Advisors' VP of Corporate Engagement. Before to joining Integrate, Ms. Powell-Rudy was an executive recruiter for a retained global search firm focused on VP through CEO level searches. Prior to working in executive recruitment, Ms. Powell-Rudy worked in technology and telecommunications in both management and staff positions in a variety of functions. Ms. Powell-Rudy graduated *summa cum laude* from Manhattanville College and has an MS in telecommunications management from NYU Polytechnic School of Engineering. She is the parent of a young adult daughter with autism.

Acknowledgments

In 2017, we wrote *An Employer's Guide to Managing Professionals on the Autism Spectrum*. At that time, autism hiring programs targeting professionals had recently been launched by a handful of Fortune 500 companies, and employers were hungry for information on how to provide a supportive work environment for their autistic and neurodivergent employees. Since then, many more organizations have launched neurodiversity and/or autism hiring programs, yet most of them are still relatively small. Even the early programs have not reached their targeted headcount levels, with many companies finding it difficult to recruit and hire neurodivergent individuals. Given this apparent mismatch between employers' struggle to "find" neurodivergent employees and the continuing high under-employment and unemployment rates among autistic professionals, we decided a book focused on practices to recruit, interview, and onboard neurodivergent and autistic talent was timely.

No book like this gets written without the help and support of a team of people. I would like to thank my co-author Joan Bogden. Joan is an invaluable editor, researcher, and taskmaster. Without her incredible executive functioning skills that kept us well organized, her insistence that the world needed this book, and her overall good humor, I am sure on multiple occasions I would have shelved this project. I also want to thank Tracy Powell-Rudy. Not only has Tracy helped me build Integrate Autism Employment Advisors (Integrate) from the ground up, as contributing author to this book she gave her expertise gleaned through her years as an Executive Recruiter prior to Integrate, her nine-plus years with Integrate, and her experience as the mother of a daughter on the spectrum and as a recently diagnosed autistic woman herself. Particularly important to the writing of this book was the input of Erich Buchrieser, Integrate's Program Administrator and an autistic advocate. Erich taught us a great deal about the use of language and helped us frame the discussions around neurodiversity, neurodivergence, and autism. Finally, I want to thank Lynda Geller, PhD. Lynda has provided her professional knowledge to Integrate from the start and was a critical reader of this book prior to publication.

Were it not for the autism community, we would not have had the experience to write this book. Over the past ten years, we've had the privilege of hearing the stories of hundreds of autistic jobseekers and learned so much from them in terms of what could be done to make the job search process work for them. Quotes from some of these individuals are included throughout the book, as their voice is the most important one to drive the message home that most recruiting and interviewing practices do not work for autistic individuals. We thank them for sharing their experiences with us and their permission to share them with you.

I'd also like to thank the many employers that have worked with Integrate over the past ten years. While Integrate's vision of inclusive, competitive employment for autistic professionals is still a work in progress, we are heartened by the efforts of each and every one of you. We have implemented many of the strategies discussed in this book with you and seen the positive impacts.

Lastly, I want to thank my son and my husband. My son because he has taught me more about autism than he will ever know. My husband because he graciously spent almost every pandemic weekend alone while I wrote this book.

Marcia Scheiner
March 2021

Introduction

A major milestone in the autism hiring movement occurred in March 2013 when SAP, the global enterprise software and technology company, announced its intention to have 1% of its workforce be composed of autistic employees by 2020. Since then, many large-scale, corporate employers (over 50 in the US as of the end of 2020 by our latest count) have embarked on some type of formal autism hiring effort, mostly targeting professional hires. Additionally, over a dozen entrepreneurs have founded companies (both nonprofit and for-profit) with a social mission of employing autistic individuals exclusively or almost exclusively. Despite these efforts, the 85% under-employment and unemployment rate for autistic college graduates has barely moved in the past eight years.[1]

Some of the companies hiring autistic talent have indicated they would have hired more professional-level employees on the spectrum by now if they could "find them". In 2019, a group of employers with established autism hiring programs published the *Autism@Work Playbook*[2] in which they noted that the most critical factor to the success of an Autism@Work program is the ability to source talent. As these employers have learned, traditional recruiting and interviewing practices are not well-suited to attracting and screening autistic talent. Additionally, the US vocational rehabilitation (VR) system is a state-based system, preventing national employers from accessing one central database to find and hire employees with any type of disability.

Not everyone with autism, particularly college graduates, registers with their state VR agency. And being registered with one's state VR agency doesn't guarantee that the agency will be aware of and have access to the types of job opportunities that are appropriate for that individual (i.e., those with a bachelor's, master's, or another professional degree) or will have the types of candidates being sought by local employers. So, an employer looking for autistic talent needs to be incredibly resourceful when seeking candidates.

In 2017, we wrote *An Employer's Guide to Managing Professionals on the Autism Spectrum* to address employers' needs in supporting existing autistic employees. At that time, Autism@Work programs were just launching, usually with small pilot groups, and employers needed guidance on creating a supportive and inclusive workplace for their autistic colleagues. As employers grow their autism hiring programs, we now feel it is important for them to have a guide to allow them to become self-sufficient in that most critical factor – the ability to source talent. In this book, we provide guidance on recruiting, interviewing, and onboarding practices that will enable employers to identify, attract, and hire qualified, autistic talent.

How to Use This Book

This book is meant to be used as a guide for employers to develop autism-friendly recruiting practices, policies, and procedures that will attract autistic professionals. In order to do so, a baseline of understanding certain core issues related to neurodiversity and the neurodivergent community, which encompasses autism, is critical. Chapter 1 discusses some of those issues and should be read in its entirety.

For those of you still considering whether to engage in an autism hiring effort, Chapters 2 and 3 provide information about the benefits autistic employees bring to their employers and what practices, procedures, and programs other organizations have implemented to attract and retain employees on the spectrum, respectively. Don't skip those chapters if you are building a case for your own organization to launch an autism hiring initiative.

Chapters 4 and 5 introduce key concepts critical to understanding the autistic jobseeker's experience. These concepts will appear time and again throughout the book to explain their impact on autistic individuals during the recruiting, interviewing, and onboarding process. It is important to read these chapters before moving onto Parts II, III, and IV, which provide specific guidance on recruiting, interviewing, and onboarding, respectively. These parts can be read as a whole or used as a reference guide as needed.

Throughout the book you will find quotes from autistic professionals who shared their interviewing and work experiences with us. Their perspectives are included to provide the reader with an autistic voice on some of the topics being discussed. These individuals are all in different stages of their careers and come from fields as diverse as human resource compliance, financial compliance, technology, and health care. Additionally, the manuscript for this book was reviewed by autistic individuals employed by Integrate Autism Employment Advisors. Please see the acknowledgments section for further information on their contribution to this book.

This book is meant to be used as a reference guide. We expect that readers will find parts of the book relevant at different times and will re-visit certain sections when necessary. As a result, you may notice that some information is repeated in various chapters of the book. This is done to allow the reader the flexibility of reading shorter segments of the book when looking for advice on a specific topic. We have provided a glossary as well as cross-references to other chapters for additional information on relevant topics to make navigating the book as efficient as possible for the reader.

Lastly, when writing this book, it was sometimes necessary to generalize, so we have included boxes, similar to the one below, in key places throughout the book:

> Not all autistic individuals will present the same. No two individuals on the spectrum are affected by autism the same way, and the behaviors they demonstrate related to autism will be unique to them.

It is important to remember that each autistic jobseeker is a unique individual looking for a challenging and rewarding employment opportunity. In that sense, they are no different than other jobseekers, autistic or not, and should be accorded the same level of consideration and respect in the job search process.

Notes

1 Hurley-Hanson, Amy E., and Cristina M. Giannantonio. "Autism in the Workplace (Special Issue)." *Journal of Business and Management* 22, no. 1 (2016): 10. https://www.chapman.edu/business/_files/journals-and-essays/jbm-e ditions/JBM-vol-22-no-1-Autism-in-the-Workplace.pdf.
2 Annabi, Hala, E. W. Crooks, Neil Barnett, J. Guadagno, James R. Mahoney, J. Michelle, A. Pacilio, Hiren Shukla, and Jose Velasco. *Autism @ Work Playbook: Finding Talent and Creating Meaningful Employment Opportunities for People with Autism*. Seattle, WA: ACCESS-IT, The Information School, University of Washington, 2019.

Part I

Understanding the Essentials

Chapter 1

What Should I Know to Get Started?

In 1997, Apple unveiled an advertising campaign around the concept that throughout history people have gone against the grain and thought differently – and implied that Apple made tools for the kinds of people who "think different". A montage of still black-and-white portraits celebrated visionaries like Albert Einstein, Thomas Edison, Pablo Picasso, Gandhi, and others we associate with innovation, creativity, and social justice, while Richard Dreyfuss narrated:

> Here's to the crazy ones.
> The misfits …
> The round pegs in the square holes.
> The ones who see the world differently …[1]

The critically acclaimed "Think Different" campaign proved to be an enormous success for Apple and marked the beginning of its re-emergence as a marketing powerhouse that, according to Apple visionary Steve Jobs, "opened up a computer world for a lot of people who thought differently".[2]

Around the same time, Australian sociologist and autism rights advocate Judy Singer coined the term "neurodiversity" (a blending of "neurological" and "diversity") to articulate the needs of people with autism who did not want to be defined by a disability label but wished to be seen instead as neurologically different.[3] In 1998, journalist and autism activist Harvey Blume introduced the concept to a broad audience when he wrote in *The Atlantic,* "Neurodiversity may be every bit as crucial for the human race as biodiversity is for life in general. Who can say what form of wiring will prove best at any given moment?"[4]

Today, this idea of neurodiversity, that there is a natural variation in how the brain works and interprets information across people, has made its way into the workplace. If you're reading this book, your organization wants to increase the number of neurodivergent employees in your workforce. Or maybe your organization is thinking about launching a targeted neurodiversity or autism hiring effort, and you want to learn the secrets to finding and recruiting neurodivergent, or more specifically, autistic candidates. Either way, you are reading this book because you want to employ talent that "thinks different". Regardless of your reasons for reading this book, the strategies recommended for recruiting, interviewing, and onboarding candidates can have a positive impact on all of the individuals you seek to hire. Most of what we recommend focuses on clear communication and strategies for unbiased assessments of applicants' skill sets.

Understanding the background of the neurodiversity movement and the issues that are important to autistic candidates is the first step to effectively attracting and retaining neurodivergent employees. This chapter will introduce you to the neurodiversity movement, provide an understanding of the use of language in the neurodivergent and autistic communities, and discuss issues surrounding disclosure.

> As you learn about neurodiversity and autism, keep in mind that no two individuals on the spectrum are affected by autism the same way, and the behaviors they demonstrate related to autism will be unique to them.

The Myth of the "Normal" Brain

"Average", "standard", and "normal" are part of a concept we apply every day – from height to IQ, blood pressure, and even clothing sizes – to make sense of the world around us. Naturally-occurring ranges of values, when plotted on a graph, are surprisingly similar and will generally follow a bell-shaped curve (Figure 1.1), a common feature of the *normal distribution* in statistics that is used to model variations in nature and human traits in psychology.

When describing human traits, the normal distribution predicts that about two-thirds (68%) of the people in a sample will fall within the "average" range, with fewer people represented at the extremes. For example, if we randomly sampled the IQ of 1,000 individuals, the average score would be 100 and we would expect 680 people to have IQs in the range of 85–115. Fewer and fewer people will be represented as their IQ scores get further away from 100 in either direction.

Our society skews toward what is considered normal or average. If the average women's shoe size is a seven, a shoe store is likely to carry more styles in sizes five to nine than in size 11, as anyone with larger-than-average feet knows. Similarly, it is impossible to plot the complexity and variety of

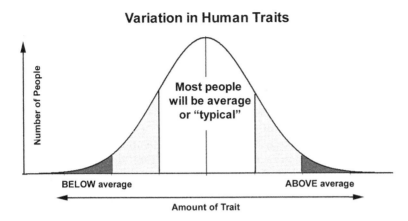

Figure 1.1 The Bell-Shaped Curve of a Normal Distribution.

human cognitive and processing styles, yet in many ways society assumes that there is a standard or "typical" way of thinking, and tends to accommodate the people who fall into that camp. In reality, while there is no one "normal" way of thinking, most people assume that others process information the same way they do, if they ever think of it at all. As a result, those whose brains work differently can face significant barriers.

Neurodiversity 101

In defining neurodiversity, Judy Singer, who is on the autism spectrum herself, wanted to reframe the discussion around diagnoses, such as autism, away from the deficits typically associated with them to a more positive discussion of the strengths that can come with an autism diagnosis, such as:

- Extreme focus and attention to detail
- Accuracy on repetitive tasks
- Pattern recognition
- Logical thinking
- High productivity
- Innovative solutions to problems

While the initial focus of neurodiversity was on autism spectrum disorder (ASD), over time the term came to encompass a number of diagnoses including attention deficit disorder (ADD), attention deficit hyperactivity disorder (ADHD), dyslexia, dyspraxia, Tourette's syndrome, dyscalculia, and obsessive-compulsive disorder (OCD), among others. The goal of the neurodiversity movement was to shift people's thinking about these conditions away from considering them deficits, disorders, or impairments toward an acceptance of them as naturally occurring facts of nature similar to biodiversity, the variety of life on Earth at all its levels.

Today, we think even more broadly when we use the term "neurodiversity":

> Humanity is neurodiverse, just as humanity is racially, ethnically, and culturally diverse. By definition, no human being falls outside of the spectrum of human neurodiversity, just as no human being falls outside of the spectrum of human racial, ethnic, and cultural diversity.[5]

Because the cognitive functioning of every individual is different, we are a *neurodiverse* society. However, as a society we do have certain behavioral expectations and norms. Individuals who process information and react to their environment in ways that allow them to meet those expectations and norms have a neurologically typical cognitive profile and are referred to as *neurotypical*. Those individuals with brains that behave differently (autism, ADHD, dyslexia, etc.), causing them to diverge significantly from those standards, are referred to as *neurodivergent*.

It is important to remember that neurodiversity implies a society that is by nature diverse (see Figure 1.2), comprising both neurotypical and

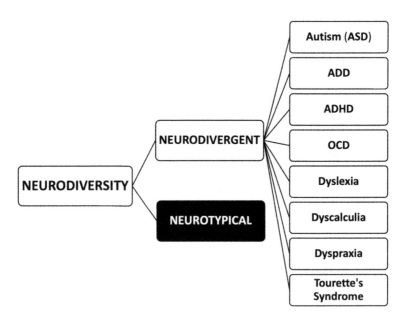

Figure 1.2 Neurodiversity Terms.

neurodivergent thinkers. *Neurodivergence* itself is diverse as well, and is made up of smaller groups, or *neurominorities*, such as autism.

The Language of Neurodiversity

The terminology around neurodiversity can be confusing. Hiring programs targeted at individuals with autism, ADD, ADHD, dyslexia, and other types of learning differences have included the terms "autism", "neurodiversity", and "neurodiverse" in their labels. In the context of the work environment, a few basic rules can be applied to ensure the correct usage of these terms. First, neurodiversity, on a stand-alone basis, is the idea that there are biological differences in all human minds. It is not a characteristic of any one individual.

Second, while neurodiverse generally refers to the neurological variations of a group, some researchers, writers, and advocates also use it to refer to a neurodivergent individual. Even online dictionaries differ in how to describe a person who is not neurotypical. In the US, the *Merriam-Webster Dictionary* does not list neurodivergent as an entry, defining "having, relating to, or constituting a type of brain functioning that is not neurotypical" as "neurodiverse".[6] The UK's *Cambridge Dictionary* defines the same as "neurodivergent", while the *Oxford Dictionary* cites both words. Throughout this book, we will refer to individuals who are not neurotypical as neurodivergent and groups as neurodiverse.

Third, autistic and neurodiverse (or neurodivergent) are not necessarily interchangeable terms:

- An autistic individual is neurodivergent, but a neurodivergent individual may not necessarily be autistic.
- The term neurotypical refers to someone who is not neurodivergent; however, a person who is not autisic is not necessarily neurotypical as they may be neurodivergent in another way.[7]

The Language of Autism

In all areas of society today, we see changes in how people use language to describe themselves and others. A heightened sense of awareness of how someone wants to be referred to in terms of their gender identity, race, religion, national origin, sexual orientation, etc., is occurring in our workplaces. This sensitivity to the use of language is no different for people who are neurodivergent and/or autistic.

Autism Spectrum Disorder

As the understanding of autism grows, the development of how we use language to refer to autistic individuals continues to evolve. The term "autism" was first used by the Swiss psychiatrist Eugen Bleuler in 1910, followed by Hans Asperger in 1938, with Leo Kanner bringing it to the US in 1943. It wasn't until the 1980s that autism became an official diagnosis in the *Diagnostic and Statistical Manual of Mental Disorders* (DSM), the official guide used by psychologists and psychiatrists in the US to diagnose and treat clients. Over the years, several related diagnoses, including Asperger syndrome, Rett syndrome, pervasive developmental disorder – not otherwise specified (PDD-NOS), and childhood disintegrative disorder (CDD), have been included in the DSM. In May 2013, the DSM-5 consolidated these related diagnoses with autism under the broader category of *autism spectrum disorder* (ASD). Additionally, during this time, in order to differentiate between those with ASD who have an intellectual disability and those who do not, the terms "high functioning" and "low functioning" came into use in the autism community.

Low Functioning vs. High Functioning

Currently, much discussion is occurring within the autism community with regard to issues surrounding the terminology used to describe autism. Most people in the autism community no longer use the terms low and high functioning. As interventions and support systems for autistic individuals have developed, it has become clear that certain characteristics, like lack of verbal language or an IQ less than 70, don't necessarily result in someone being low functioning. Conversely, expressive language and an IQ over 70 do not make someone high functioning. Not only do many more factors need to be considered to assess an individual's functioning level, but people also grow and change over time. The high/low assessment does not provide a meaningful descriptor of an individual's abilities yet it can perpetuate harmful stereotypes, stigmatize, and cause severe emotional distress for individuals and their families.

Person-First vs. Identity-First

Another debate in the autism community concerns the use of person-first versus identity-first language. For those of you unfamiliar with these terms, in the case of disability, *person-first language* puts the person before the disability, e.g., "person with autism", while "autistic person" is an example of *identity-first language*. In a blog published by the Autistic Self-Advocacy Network, a national disability rights organization by and for autistic individuals, the author argues in favor of identity-first language saying, "When we say 'person with autism', we say that it is unfortunate and an accident that a person is Autistic … when we say, 'Autistic person', we recognize, affirm, and validate an individual's identity as an Autistic person".[8]

To address the language preferences of autistic individuals in this book, we use a combination of person-first and identity-first language, with a preponderance of identity-first usage. We mostly use the term autistic for identity-first references but we also use neurodivergent when the practices we are discussing are applicable to both categories of individuals. For person-first language we use autism and on the *spectrum*, as the official diagnosis for autistic individuals is autism spectrum disorder. Just as the use of personal pronouns is now standard business practice, as you embark on hiring neurodivergent and autistic employees, be mindful of your use of language. Ask candidates their preference for person-first or identity-first language if the topic arises.[9]

"*Nothing About Us Without Us*" is an important idea in the autism community that means autistic people should be involved whenever autism is discussed. As authors, we are not neurodivergent ourselves but have had autistic individuals read our manuscript and check our use of language. If you already have neurodivergent and autistic employees, engage them in reviewing your hiring processes and how you present and implement any efforts around autism and neurodiversity hiring.

Disclosure

In our previous book, *An Employer's Guide to Managing Professionals on the Autism Spectrum* (Jessica Kingsley Publishers, 2017), we devote an entire chapter to disclosure and its benefits for employers. When managing autistic employees, knowing they have a disability can be an advantage in providing them with what they need to be successful at work. The same is true when recruiting and interviewing neurodivergent and autistic job candidates. One of the biggest obstacles for autistic individuals in obtaining work is the interview process. As an employer, you can provide opportunities for potential candidates to disclose, offering them an appropriate and positive interview experience where they can demonstrate their skill sets and talents, and become a contributing member of your organization.

Most employers know (and if they don't, should) that it is illegal to ask a job applicant or an employee if they have a disability. Furthermore, if an employer knows someone has a disability, it is illegal to ask about the severity of that disability.[10] In March 2014, the US Department of Labor's Office of Federal Contract Compliance Programs (OFCCP) amended Section 503 of the Rehabilitation Act of 1973 to require all federal contractors to provide job applicants with the ability to self-identify as having a disability during the pre-offer stage of the hiring process.[11] As a result, many employers chose to add a question about disability to their job application where a candidate could respond yes or no, if they choose to do so. While this information allows employers to track data on the number of disclosed applicants with some form of disability, it does not provide employers with any information that allows them to support candidates with accommodations they may require during the recruiting and interview process. Unless the candidate discloses further, including the specifics of their disability, the individuals involved in the hiring process will typically not even know the candidate has a disability.

Yet according to the Center for Disease Control, 26% of the adult population has a disability[12] and half of those are individuals with hidden or *invisible disabilities.*[13] If one in every ten (or 10%) job applicants has an invisible disability, and as an employer you are not attracting these candidates, or worse yet, your recruiting and interview process is screening them out, you are missing out on a significant segment of the workforce. But if you are not allowed to ask job candidates about specific disabilities, how can you convey to applicants that you are an equal opportunity employer who wants to provide an inclusive interview and work experience to all employees, particularly for those with disabilities? While the focus of this book is on creating a recruiting and interviewing process that would encourage autistic candidates to disclose, the techniques suggested below (as discussed in Chapter 7) readily apply to all candidates who may have a hidden disability.

- Ask all candidates what they might want: The process of interviewing can be intimidating, whether someone has a disability or not. Ask all candidates, *prior to their scheduled interview,* if there is any information they want to have shared with their interviewers and/or any accommodations provided to them as part of the interview process.
- Leverage your website: On your company's website, feature a landing page expressly for candidates with disabilities. Provide concrete information on your organization's practices and policies for jobseekers and employees seeking accommodations. If you have specific programs supporting employees with disabilities (e.g., an Autism@Work program), highlight those programs and provide contact information for candidates. If your company has employee resource groups (ERGs) or business resource groups (BRGs) for employees with an interest in or who identify with certain groups, including those with disabilities, again, highlight the availability of those groups on your website. Provide information on how to contact these groups so prospective candidates can learn about the prevalence of people with disabilities in your organization and the culture they may encounter.
- Publicize your support for inclusion: If you have specific programs supporting employees with disabilities, your website shouldn't be the only place you highlight these programs. Let the market know about these efforts through professional associations, trade organizations, job fairs, business publications, any place jobseekers may be looking for career opportunities. Set up social media sites targeted to disability audiences that share your organization's values and vision for an inclusive workplace and a link to your careers site.

The legal interpretation of the ADA supports the creation of neurodivergent/autism-specific hiring programs, allowing employers to have a distinct hiring process for individuals with a designated disability. If the candidate has voluntarily disclosed by applying through such a program, once the employer has made an offer of employment, the employer can ask the candidates about their disability prior to commencing employment, if they do so for all candidates.[14] Some candidates will prefer to be part of a designated autism hiring effort and others will want to participate in your standard process, with possible accommodations. If your organization offers an option to applicants, ask candidates which they prefer and discuss the pros and cons with them.

Lastly, some candidates will voluntarily disclose during an interview that they are on the autism spectrum or are neurodivergent. Should a candidate disclose to you, the appropriate response is to thank them for sharing the information and ask if they have any additional information or requests they want to make at that time. If you are not as familiar with autism as you would like to be, you can ask the candidate to tell you more about how autism may affect how they will present during the interview or their job performance. Remember, however, it will be at the candidate's discretion as to the depth of information they choose to share during the interview.

Conclusion

Effectively attracting and retaining employees on the spectrum requires an understanding of the issues that are important to autistic candidates. There is no one "normal" brain, and the neurodiversity movement reframed the diagnosis of autism and other neurodivergent conditions from a medical model of deficits to the diversity of cognitive styles and thinking that reflect the natural variation of all living species. Given that the customs and practices of societies are constantly changing, it is not out of the realm of possibility that today's neurodivergent thinker may be tomorrow's neurotypical candidate and vice versa.

Two issues of critical importance to the neurodivergent and autistic communities are the language surrounding autism and creating an environment for disclosure. While our focus in this book is on employment and the workplace, neurodivergent candidates may deal with issues of how to talk about their diagnoses or whether to disclose in almost every facet of their lives. As an employer, your awareness of these issues is key, as is how your organization approaches them for the autism community.

Notes

1 Renesi, Marianna. "Think Different: A Flashback of an Historical Campaign." *Medium*, March 25, 2018. https://medium.com/ad-discovery-and-creativity-lab/think-different-b566c2e6117f.

2 Renesi, Marianna, "Think Different".
3 Armstrong, Thomas. "The Myth of the Normal Brain: Embracing Neurodiversity." *AMA Journal of Ethics* 17 (April 23, 2015): 348–352. https://doi.org/10.1001/j ournalofethics.2015.17.4.msoc1-1504.
4 Blume, Harvey. "Neurodiversity: On the Neurological Underpinnings of Geekdom." The *Atlantic*, September 30, 1998. https://www.theatlantic.com/ma gazine/archive/1998/09/neurodiversity/305909/.
5 Walker, Nick. "Neurodiversity: Some Basic Terms & Definitions." *Neurocosmopolitanism*, September 27, 2014. https://neurocosmopolitanism.c om/neurodiversity-some-basic-terms-definitions/.
6 Merriam-Webster Dictionary. s.v. "Neurodiverse." February 8, 2021. https://ww w.merriam-webster.com/dictionary/neurodiverse.
7 Walker, Nick, "Neurodiversity".
8 Brown, Lydia. "Identity-First Language." Autistic Self Advocacy Network. July 11, 2021. https://autisticadvocacy.org/about-asan/identity-first-language/.
9 Bulluss, Erin, and Abby Sesterka. "Talking about Autism: Why Language Matters." *Psychology Today*, October 1, 2019. https://www.psychologytoday.co m/blog/insights-about-autism/201910/talking-about-autism.
10 US Equal Employment Opportunity Commission. "Your Employment Rights as an Individual with a Disability." May 19, 2020. https://www.eeoc.gov/facts/ ada18.html.
11 PolicyWorks. "The Business Case for Hiring Workers with Disabilities." March 8, 2021. http://toolkit.disabilitypolicyworks.org/the-business-case-for-hiring-workers-with-disabilities/.
12 CDC. "Disability Impacts All of Us Infographic." *Centers for Disease Control and Prevention*, March 8, 2019. https://www.cdc.gov/ncbddd/disabilityandhealt h/infographic-disability-impacts-all.html.
13 Disabled World. "Invisible Disabilities: List and General Information." November 8, 2019. https://www.disabled-world.com/disability/types/invisible/.
14 Bernick, Michael S. "Putting Autism to Work." *ChiefExecutive.Net* (blog), February 13, 2020. https://chiefexecutive.net/creating-a-targeted-neurodiversity -employment-initiative/.

Chapter 2

Why Hire Autistic Professionals?

As a recruiter, hiring manager, or diversity and inclusion professional, your success is measured by your ability to attract and retain talent. With a US labor force of over 164 million people at the beginning of 2020,[1] one would think it would be easy to find qualified individuals to fill almost any job. In the months immediately after the onset of COVID-19, unemployment rates jumped from 3.5% to the mid-teens. Yet, once employers adjusted to the pandemic and resumed hiring, finding the right person for the job could still be difficult. However, a largely untapped pool of candidates can be found in the autism community.

In the US today, one in every 54 eight-year-olds is diagnosed with an autism spectrum disorder[2] and 5.4 million adults[3] are estimated to be autistic. While 2.2% of adults living in the US have autism, their employment outcomes are far worse than those for individuals with other disabilities. By the time they are in their twenties, only 58% of autistic individuals will have had some form of paid employment, compared to 74% for those with intellectual disabilities, 91% for those with a speech impairment or emotional disturbance, and 95% for those with a learning disability.[4] For the 35%[5] of autistic individuals who attend college, their employment outcomes are even worse than their non-college-educated autistic peers, with unemployment and underemployment rates estimated to be 85%.[6] Based on these numbers, hundreds of thousands of autistic individuals are available for employment.

Hiring neurodivergent employees drives better business performance, provides broad economic benefits, and creates positive societal outcomes: these are compelling reasons to add autistic professionals to your workforce. In this chapter you'll see how a neurodiversity hiring program can increase the bottom line for companies, reduce the cost of social services borne by taxpayers, and improve the mental health of neurodivergent individuals and their families.

Business Benefits

We've all heard senior leaders say, "our organization is only as good as its people" or "our most valuable assets go home every night". Many employers spend a lot of time and money investing in human capital in the belief that it delivers economic value for the organization and its stakeholders. Autistic individuals can bring unique skill sets to their job as well as create broader benefits for an organization, such as increased productivity and employee engagement, lower turnover, and greater brand recognition.

Talents

While every person on the spectrum is different, it is not uncommon for autistic individuals to pursue with extreme devotion a subject that is their passion. In the workplace, this may present as an employee who is a subject matter expert, having a depth of knowledge exceeding that of anyone else. According to a software engineer on the spectrum:

> Whenever there was some kind of problem or something that wasn't working properly, people would come to me and ask me to look and see if I could find what the problem was ... If something didn't work, I would ... "bang my head against the wall", until I finally found the problems.

This depth of knowledge, laser-like focus, and attention to detail are recognized as hallmarks of autistic employees, though they can be accompanied by struggles with multi-tasking or shifting quickly from one task to another. (For strategies on managing these characteristics in autistic employees, see our companion book, *An Employer's Guide to Managing Professionals on the Autism Spectrum.*)

Keep in mind that just as with neurotypical candidates, it is important not to assume that all autistic candidates are the same in their skill sets, talents, capabilities, and challenges related to autism.

Most importantly, autistic individuals think differently than their neurotypical peers. This oftentimes brings a unique perspective to their work that can result in innovation and creative problem-solving, as noted in a 2017 *Harvard Business Review* article entitled "Neurodiversity as a Competitive Advantage":

> At HPE (Hewlett Packard Enterprise), neurodiverse software testers observed that one client's projects always seemed to go into crisis mode before a launch. Intolerant of disorder, they strenuously questioned the company's apparent acceptance of the chaos. This led the client company to realize that it had indeed become too tolerant of these crises and, with the help of the testers, to successfully redesign the launch

process. At SAP, a global enterprise software and technology company, a neurodiverse customer support analyst spotted an opportunity to let customers help solve a common problem themselves; thousands of them subsequently used the resources he created.[7]

Increased Productivity

Focus, attention to detail, accuracy, ability to memorize facts and figures, and enjoying routine are common characteristics of autistic individuals. These, coupled with a strong work ethic and moral code, result in employees who are typically interested in completing their assigned tasks and staying busy on the job. Rarely does an employer complain about an autistic employee spending too much time socializing on the job. As a result, they are often highly productive employees. James Mahoney, the former Global Head of Autism at Work at JPMorgan Chase, states, "Our autistic employees achieve, on average, 48% to 140% more work than their typical colleagues, depending on the roles".[8] Remember, this is an average, and not all autistic employees will, nor should they be expected to, perform at a higher productivity rate than their neurotypical peers.

Lower Turnover

Change can be anxiety producing for anyone. For individuals on the spectrum, who have often struggled to find a job, moving to a new employer can be particularly stressful. Once in an organization where they are successful and feel valued, many autistic people will prefer to stay with that same employer rather than experience the anxiety associated with a move. Additionally, they tend to be loyal to those managers and colleagues with whom they have established trust and solid working relationships. So, providing an environment where autistic employees can be comfortable "bringing their whole selves to work" and knowing they can have a meaningful career will engender loyalty.

As a manager, avoiding the extra work (training and disruption) associated with turnover is attractive; the cost savings of lower turnover are also significant. Depending on the level of the position to be filled, studies have shown that it can cost from 16% of annual salary to fill high-turnover, low-paying jobs, up to nine months of annual salary for manager-level positions.[9]

Employee Engagement

Forbes defines *employee engagement* as "the emotional commitment the employee has to the organization and its goals".[10] Engaged employees are less likely to leave your organization and are more productive when they are at work. Studies show that companies with higher employee engagement experience 16% greater profitability, 37% lower absenteeism, an

18% increase in productivity, and up to a 65% reduction in turnover: this can translate into two and a half times higher revenue. Yet, according to Gallup, only 15% of employees around the world are fully engaged in their jobs.[11] So how does hiring autistic talent help employers improve employee engagement?

With one in 54 children diagnosed as autistic and 2.2% of adults in the US on the autism spectrum, almost all organizations employ autistic people – diagnosed and undiagnosed – or have employees who have a personal connection to autism. Whether that connection is as a parent, grandparent, other family member, spouse, or friend, each of these employees wants to see the autistic person they know succeed. When they witness their employer's efforts to hire and support autistic employees, it confirms that the company's values around neurodiversity reflect a shared goal: to see greater opportunities for the people in their lives who are on the spectrum. This "emotional commitment" contributes to greater employee engagement.

Brand Recognition

Hiring autistic individuals can increase your company's brand recognition and market share. In their annual Purpose Biometrics Study, Porter Novelli/ Cone found that 79% of Americans want companies to support issues that are personally important to them, and 86% say they are likely to purchase products and services from these companies.[12] The Center for Disease Control currently estimates that approximately 6.78 million autistic children and adults are living in the US, while The Return on Disability Group estimates that every person with a disability in the US has 1.85 family members/friends.[13] Even by a conservative estimate, this is an extended "autism market" of 12.5 million people or 3.8% of the US population – a significant market share for any company.

A customer's personal connection to autism can be a deciding factor in which brand or service to choose. For example, within a one-block radius of our offices in New York City are four multinational banks, all offering largely the same services. As I am the parent of an autistic son, our organization patronizes the bank that has the most robust autism hiring initiative.

Tax Credits

Government programs targeted at encouraging employers to hire people with disabilities provide tax credits to small and large businesses at the federal and state level. At the federal level, small businesses earning $1 million or less or with 30 or fewer employees may be eligible for the Disabled Access Credit, ranging anywhere from $250 to $10,000; all employers may be eligible for the Workforce Opportunity Tax Credit, ranging from $1,200 to $9,600 per employee, depending on the employee hired and the length of employment.[14] Every state differs in what they offer, so employers should check with their local tax authorities for advice.

Regulatory Compliance

If you are a federal contractor, keep in mind that hiring autistic individuals and creating an environment that encourages disclosure of neurodivergent employees will help toward compliance with Section 503 of the Rehabilitation Act of 1973 issued by the US Office of Federal Contract Compliance Programs (OFCCP). For employers subject to these guidelines, the OFCCP recently revised the requirements for the Voluntary Self-Identification of Disability form employers must provide all applicants and current employees.[15] The form must now include a disclosure statement saying, "We are also required to measure our progress toward having at least 7% of our workforce be individuals with disabilities".[16] One of the best practices listed by the Department of Labor for meeting the 7% target is the introduction of disability inclusion programs,[17] such as a dedicated autism hiring effort.

Economic Benefits

Autistic individuals have dreams and desires for an independent, productive life, no different from any other person. For many with autism, this goal is achievable, provided they are given the opportunities to do so. Without competitive employment, however, an independent life is out of reach. For someone with a disability who may require financial support as a result of that disability, the costs of not having employment to both society and the individual can be significant.

The US government offers two programs to provide financial support for individuals with disabilities: Social Security and Medicaid. Social security disability income (SSDI) pays, on average, $1,258.98 per month ($15,107.76 per annum).[18] SSDI is based on income, so to qualify an individual must have worked in the past and prove they have a qualifying disability that prevents them from continuing the same level of work for the long term.[19] Supplemental security income (SSI) pays up to $783 per month ($9,396 per annum).[20] To qualify for SSI, an individual needs to be disabled and unable to work at a level that is considered to be a substantial gainful activity (SGA), i.e., less than $1,260 per month.[21] In addition to SSDI or SSI, a disabled individual can qualify for free medical coverage under Medicaid. The average spending per person per year for Medicaid can range from $3,000 for an adult to over $20,000 for an individual with disabilities[22] *(see the comparison in Table 2.1).*

Due to the previous work requirement, it is often not possible for autistic individuals to qualify for SSDI. Those individuals on the spectrum who do not qualify for SSDI, however, can apply for SSI and Medicaid. These

Table 2.1 Social Security Disability Income (SSDI) vs. Supplemental Security Income (SSI)

Federal Financial Support Programs for Individuals with Disabilities

SSDI	SSI
• Work history (based on SS earning record) • $1,258/month (2020 average) • Can't continue *same level of work* as previously for one year • May also be eligible for SSI	• No work history • Up to $783/month (2020) • Not able to work at SGA level (<$1,260/month) • Nutrition: SNAP $127/month • Medicaid: $3,000 (adult) to $20,000+ (disabled)

benefits can sometimes be supplemented by additional welfare programs such as the Supplemental Nutrition Assistance Program (SNAP). The average SNAP recipient receives $127 per month.[23]

While no government data is available that calculates the cost to the US of the high unemployment rate of autistic individuals, it clearly is not insubstantial. As an example, for an autistic individual with no work history who qualifies for the maximum amount of SSI ($9,396 per year), the average amount of SNAP ($2,724), and incurs average medical (Medicaid) expenses ($10,068 per year), *the total annual government benefits paid would be $22,188.*

No data exists confirming how many autistic individuals are receiving these benefits. It is not an easy process to navigate, as demonstrated by a growing industry of consultants to guide families through the process of applying and qualifying for these government programs. However, as Figure 2.1 illustrates, for every 1% of the estimated 5.4 million adults with autism on government benefits that become employed (i.e., no longer need SSI, SNAP, and Medicaid), the yearly cost savings to these programs would be almost $1.2 billion!

For every 1% of autistic adults employed

Figure 2.1 Economic Advantage of Employing Autistic Individuals.

While not every autistic individual can be employed at a level that would exempt them from receiving government benefits, many individuals would gladly forgo them for competitive employment. For those who can come off government support programs and enter the workforce, society has the added benefit of converting them from a benefits recipient to a taxpayer.

DXC Technology, in collaboration with the Australian Government Department of Human Services, Department of Defense, and Department of Immigration and Border Protection, has developed some data around the cost savings to the Australian government of the implementation of their autism hiring initiative, known as The Dandelion Program. The analysis, completed by researchers from La Trobe University, estimated that for every 100 individuals previously unemployed and on welfare who participate in the three-year Dandelion Employment Program full-time, the program will generate AUD $2,826,600 in tax benefits, save AUD $3,219,840 in welfare payments, and potentially save AUD $600,000 in reduced use of employment services.[24] That same research report stated:

> A report commissioned by the Network on Disability suggested that a one-third reduction in the difference between employment rates for people with and without disabilities would result in an AUD $43 billion increase, and long-term rise of 0.85% in Australia's GDP.

The economic advantage for any country's economy of putting capable individuals with disabilities to work in appropriate, competitive employment is indisputable.

Societal Benefits

As children, we are taught that hard work is a reward unto itself, and research into the connection between meaningful work and mental well-being supports this. Psychologist David L. Blustein found that working is a central aspect of life and plays an important role in people's psychological health, providing a source of structure, a means of survival, connection to others, and optimally a means of self-determination.[25] For autistic individuals, J. K. Y. Lai, E. Rhee, and D. Nicholas found employment can play a role in offsetting mental health issues, such as depression and suicidality.[26] Not only is having work beneficial; *not* having work can have a negative impact on mental health. Studies show that unemployed individuals report approximately 30% more negative emotional experiences in their day-to-day lives than individuals who are working.[27]

The benefits of working go beyond improving the emotional life of the individual who is employed. Many autistic adults who are unemployed are dependent on family members for some or all of their financial support, including living with aging parents. This can impact both the self-esteem and the overall sense of well-being of the autistic individual. The employees of DXC's Dandelion program talked about the financial benefits the program has brought to their lives:

I still live with my mum because … she's not in a very well-paid job so she wouldn't be able to afford the house. So I actually, instead of becoming a financial burden, I actually became a significant augmentation to the house income.[28]

Conclusion

The potential pool of neurodivergent talent is one that is significant and largely untapped. In a world where a return on investment (ROI) is important, hiring autistic individuals is good for business. Professional candidates on the autism spectrum, with their different cognitive thinking processes, bring innovative solutions to the workplace. Their tendency to maintain a laser focus and dislike of change makes them highly productive and less likely to leave, reducing turnover. In addition to the autistic employee, family and friends are important stakeholders in the success of a business: employee engagement and market share increase as a business becomes recognized as an employer of choice for neurodivergent individuals, and federal and state tax credit programs designed specifically to encourage the employment of people with disabilities are available.

Beyond the bottom line of any individual business, hiring autistic individuals is good for our broader economy and society. Any time someone can transition from being a recipient of government support to a taxpayer, everyone benefits. Those benefits include actual dollar savings and contribution to GDP, as well as improved mental health for the individual who has become employed and the emotional and financial well-being of their family. So, the real question should be: why *not* hire autistic professionals?

Notes

1 Bureau of Labor Statistics. "Civilian Labor Force Level." *FRED, Federal Reserve Bank of St. Louis*, August 6, 2020. https://fred.stlouisfed.org/series/CLF16OV.
2 CDC. "Data and Statistics on Autism Spectrum Disorder." *Centers for Disease Control and Prevention*, March 25, 2020. https://www.cdc.gov/ncbddd/autism/data.html.
3 CDC. "CDC Releases First Estimates of the Number of Adults Living with ASD." *Centers for Disease Control and Prevention*, April 27, 2020. https://www.cdc.gov/ncbddd/autism/features/adults-living-with-autism-spectrum-disorder.html.
4 Singh, Maanvi. "Young Adults with Autism More Likely to Be Unemployed, Isolated." *NPR*, August 7, 2020. https://www.npr.org/sections/health-shots/2015/04/21/401243060/young-adults-with-autism-more-likely-to-be-unemployed-isolated.
5 Shattuck, Paul T., Sarah Carter Narendorf, Benjamin Cooper, Paul R. Sterzing, Mary Wagner, and Julie Lounds Taylor. "Postsecondary Education and Employment among Youth with an Autism Spectrum Disorder." *Pediatrics* 129, no. 6 (June 2012): 1042. https://doi.org/10.1542/peds.2011-2864.

6 Griffiths, Amy-Jane, Cristina M. Giannantonio, Amy E. Hurley-Hanson, and Donald N. Cardinal. "Autism in the Workplace: Assessing the Transition Needs of Young Adults with Autism Spectrum Disorder." *Journal of Business and Management* 22, no. 1 (2016): 5–22. https://www.chapman.edu/business/_files/journals-and-essays/jbm-editions/JBM-vol-22-no-1-Autism-in-the-   Workplace.pdf.

7 Austin, Robert D., and Gary P. Pisano. "Neurodiversity as a Competitive Advantage." *Harvard Business Review*, May 1, 2017. https://hbr.org/2017/05/neurodiversity-as-a-competitive-advantage.

8 Eng, Dinah. "Where Autistic Workers Thrive." *Fortune*, June 24, 2018. https://fortune.com/2018/06/24/where-autistic-workers-thrive/.

9 Merhar, Christina. "Employee Retention – The Real Cost of Losing an Employee." *PeopleKeep*, June 2, 2020. https://www.peoplekeep.com/blog/employee-retention-the-real-cost-of-losing-an-employee.

10 Kruse, Kevin. "What is Employee Engagement?" *Forbes*, June 22, 2012. https://www.forbes.com/sites/kevinkruse/2012/06/22/employee-engagement-what-and-why/?sh=29bd188d7f37.

11 Ginac, Linda. "Impacts on Employee Engagement with Performance Management." *HR Technologist*, September 17, 2018. https://www.hrtechnologist.com/articles/employee-engagement/impacts-on-employee-engagement-with-performance-management/.

12 Cone Communications. "Feeling Purpose: 2019 Porter Novelli/Cone Purpose Biometrics Study." 2019. https://www.conecomm.com/research-blog/purpose-biometrics.

13 Return on Disability Group. "2020 Annual Report Summary – The Global Economics of Disability." March 22, 2021. http://rod-group.com/sites/default/files/Summary%20Report%20-%20The%20Global%20Economics%20of%20Disability%202020.pdf.

14 Internal Revenue Service. "Tax Benefits for Businesses Who Have Employees with Disabilities." March 22, 2020. https://www.irs.gov/businesses/small-businesses-self-employed/tax-benefits-for-businesses-who-have-employees-with-disabilities.

15 View form at: https://www.dol.gov/sites/dolgov/files/OFCCP/regs/compliance/sec503/Self_ID_Forms/503Self-IDForm.pdf.

16 Linguist, Stacie L., and Kristin Jones Pierre. "OFCCP Revises Voluntary Self-Identification Disability Form." *The National Law Review*, May 11, 2020. https://www.natlawreview.com/article/ofccp-revises-voluntary-self-identification-disability-form.

17 US Department of Labor. "Section 503 Best Practices for Federal Contractors." August 7, 2020. https://www.dol.gov/agencies/ofccp/compliance-assistance/outreach/resources/section-503-vevraa/503.

18 Social Security Administration. "Disabled-Worker Statistics." June 2020. https://www.ssa.gov/oact/STATS/dib-g3.html.

19 Social Security Administration. "How You Qualify: Disability Benefits." August 7, 2020. https://www.ssa.gov/benefits/disability/qualify.html.

20 Social Security Administration. "SSI Federal Payment Amounts for 2020." August 7, 2020. https://www.ssa.gov/oact/cola/SSI.html.

21 Social Security Administration. "Understanding SSI – If You Are Disabled or Blind." August 7, 2020. https://www.ssa.gov/ssi/text-disable-ussi.htm#sgact.

22 Medicaid. "How Much Do States Spend Per Medicaid Enrollee?" August 7, 2020. https://www.medicaid.gov/state-overviews/scorecard/how-much-states-spend-per-medicaid-enrollee/index.html.

23 Center on Budget and Policy Priorities. "Chart Book: SNAP Helps Struggling Families Put Food on the Table." November 7, 2019. https://www.cbpp.org/rese arch/food-assistance/chart-book-snap-helps-struggling-families-put-food-on-the -table.

24 Hedley, Darren, Mathilda Wilmot, Jennifer Spoor, and Cheryl Dissanayake. "Benefits of Employing People with Autism: The Dandelion Employment Program." *DXC Dandelion Program*, 2017, 22. https://digitalcommons.ilr.cor nell.edu/dandelionprogram/25.

25 Blustein, David L. "The Role of Work in Psychological Health and Well-Being: A Conceptual, Historical, and Public Policy Perspective." *American Psychologist* 63, no. 4 (2008): 228–40. doi:10.1037/0003-066x.63.4.228.

26 Lai, Jonathan K.Y., Esther Rhee, and David Nicholas. "Suicidality in Autism Spectrum Disorder: A Commentary." *Advances In Neurodevelopmental Disorders* 1, no. 3 (2017): 190–95. doi:10.1007/s41252-017-0018-4.

27 De Neve, Jan-Emmanuel, and George Ward. "Does Work Make You Happy? Evidence from the World Happiness Report." *Harvard Business Review*, March 20, 2017. https://hbr.org/2017/03/does-work-make-you-happy-evidence-from-th e-world-happiness-report.

28 Hedley et al., "Benefits of Employing People with Autism." 9.

Chapter 3

Are Neurodiversity Hiring Programs Necessary?

The standard recruiting and interviewing processes are designed for uniformities in cognitive styles and, in particular, the ways neurotypical candidates think. Unfortunately, these practices often obscure the unique talents neurodivergent candidates can bring to an organization. While some autistic individuals do obtain employment through an employer's standard recruiting process without disclosing they have a neurodivergent profile or requesting an accommodation, the unemployment statistics for this population suggest that they are in the minority. To address this, some employers are modifying their recruiting and interviewing practices to offer autistic candidates the opportunity to demonstrate their skill sets in ways that suit their presentation styles, while others have gone as far as setting up completely distinct programs and processes for hiring autistic employees.

In this chapter, we will discuss the history of neurodiversity hiring programs, various hiring approaches, and strategies for launching your own program.

The History of Neurodiversity Hiring Programs

Present-day neurodiversity hiring programs have evolved from a combination of federal and corporate initiatives (see Figure 3.1 for a timeline of disability hiring programs). Before launching a program, it is helpful to understand this historical evolution. History has shown that the number of ways to implement an autism hiring program has grown. It is important to understand the options available and choose one or more program models that will achieve the long-term goals of your organization.

The Vocational Rehabilitation Act of 1920, which provided funds for people with *physical disabilities* for vocational guidance, training, occupational adjustment, prostheses, and placement services, laid the groundwork for the current vocational service system for people with disabilities in the US. Throughout the years, the Vocational Rehabilitation Act was expanded to include services for persons with other types of disabilities. The

History of Disability and Neurodiversity Hiring Initiatives

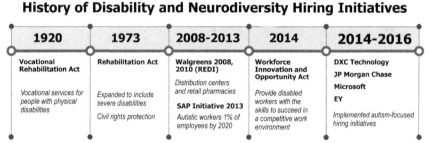

1920	1973	2008-2013	2014	2014-2016
Vocational Rehabilitation Act	**Rehabilitation Act**	**Walgreens 2008, 2010 (REDI)**	**Workforce Innovation and Opportunity Act**	**DXC Technology**
				JP Morgan Chase
		Distribution centers and retail pharmacies		**Microsoft**
Vocational services for people with physical disabilities	*Expanded to include severe disabilities*	**SAP Initiative 2013**	*Provide disabled workers with the skills to succeed in a competitive work environment*	**EY**
	Civil rights protection	*Autistic workers 1% of employees by 2020*		*Implemented autism-focused hiring initiatives*

Figure 3.1 Timeline of Disability Hiring Programs.

Rehabilitation Act of 1973 was passed to include persons with severe disabilities and incorporate civil rights protection for persons with disabilities.[1] In 2014, the laws guiding vocational services were updated with the passage of the Workforce Innovation and Opportunity Act of 2014 (WIOA). WIOA was "designed to help job seekers access employment, education, training, and support services to succeed in the labor market and to match employers with the skilled workers they need to compete in the global economy".[2] Unlike prior legislation, the intent of WIOA was to put a focus on ensuring disabled workers are provided with the skills to succeed in a competitive employment environment and engage employers in a more meaningful way in the process of creating employment opportunities for people with disabilities.

Meanwhile, on the corporate side, by 2008 Walgreen's started hiring a significant number of employees with disabilities to work in two major distribution centers, and in 2010 started the Retail Employee Disability Initiative (REDI) to train people with disabilities in their retail pharmacies. In March 2013 (a year before the passage of WIOA), SAP, the software and technology solutions company, announced its intention to have 1% of its workforce be composed of autistic employees by 2020. For a Fortune 500 company, this was an incredible commitment at that time.

With SAP's announcement, hopes were high that doors would begin opening at large employers interested in including autistic jobseekers in their ranks worldwide. SAP was followed by several other global employers in making a significant commitment to implementing autism hiring programs – DXC Technology (2014), JPMorgan Chase and Microsoft (2015), and EY (2016). Today, these five employers have the largest neurodiversity hiring efforts among multinational corporations, measured by the number of employees hired. Additionally, by our estimate, at least 50 other major corporations worldwide have launched hiring initiatives targeting a neurodivergent/autistic talent pool.

Hiring Approaches

The approaches employers take to include neurodivergent individuals in their employee ranks can range from hiring initiatives developed specifically for autistic candidates to the integration of processes within the company's existing hiring practices.

Distinct Hiring Processes

Some companies choose to establish a neurodiversity or autism hiring program that is distinct and separate from their regular recruiting and interviewing practices. These programs include screening processes developed specifically for neurodivergent individuals that require potential candidates to spend anywhere from one to several weeks in hands-on activities and team exercises at the company, to judge both their technical and work readiness skills, before determining which candidates will receive an offer of permanent employment. Individuals who do receive an offer may be hired as part of a dedicated team of specialists, working under one manager on a specific task (e.g., data analysis or software testing) or they may then be assigned to jobs within the organization. These multi-week screening programs can be run by the employer or by third-party organizations hired to assist with the process.

Integrated Hiring Processes

Other companies choose to integrate their neurodiversity hiring efforts into their existing recruiting and interviewing practices. This entails detailed reviews of current recruiting and interviewing practices to make modifications appropriate for neurodivergent candidates. Some of the key areas of focus in such a review would include:

- Reviewing current diversity and inclusion practices related to people with disabilities
- Determining appropriate open roles available for neurodivergent candidates
- Writing "autism-friendly" job descriptions
- Reviewing the interview process for recommended modifications, including a review of questions, the inclusion of skills-based testing, and the determination of appropriate interview formats (e.g., individual interviews, panel interviews, full days of interviews including lunch, etc.)
- Determining training needed for recruiters, hiring managers, and other staff to ensure they know how to create an appropriate interview experience for neurodivergent candidates

Autistic and neurodivergent individuals hired through this approach go through an employer's typical recruiting and interviewing process, allowing for customized modifications based on each candidate's needs, with the goal of obtaining a fully integrated role in the organization.

Regardless of which model an employer chooses, the hiring of the candidate is just the beginning. All successful models include structured ongoing support for both the autistic employees and their managers. In Chapters 12–15 we will cover some of the critical areas of support when onboarding neurodivergent talent. For additional information on managing autistic employees, see our companion book, *An Employer's Guide to Managing Professionals on the Autism Spectrum.*

Specialized Companies

In addition to large corporations seeing the value in hiring autistic talent, a number of specialized companies, founded specifically to hire predominantly neurodivergent professionals, have been started by autistic individuals, family members of those on the spectrum, and business entrepreneurs. Many of these companies, such as Ultranauts, Daivergent, Iterators, Autonomy Works, MindShift, Aspiritech, and Auticon, focus on technology-related jobs, so may not be an option for many individuals on the spectrum who have developed expertise in other fields.

Keeping It Legal

As more and more companies consider targeted autism and neurodiversity employment initiatives, some employers question whether the establishment of separate recruiting programs and practices to attract an identified class of individuals is discriminatory. The Americans with Disabilities Act of 1990 (ADA) specifically addresses this concern. According to employment and labor lawyer Michael Bernick, the ADA "does not explicitly prohibit a distinct hiring process for workers with autism or other defined neurological conditions".[3] In other words, the creation of hiring initiatives targeted at workers with specific disabilities does not violate disability employment laws. However, keep in mind that separately defined programs aimed at recruiting neurodivergent and/or autistic employees must still comply with ADA requirements, such as equal pay, job assignments, training, and reasonable accommodations.

Where Do You Find Autistic Talent?

With all this hiring activity over the past eight years, the frustrating reality for the autism community is that the unemployment rate for autistic individuals has not seen any noticeable improvement. Even those companies with the most developed autism hiring programs will admit that at times they struggle to find autistic talent to fill open roles. This challenge is driven by two factors. First, many of the opportunities being identified for autistic candidates today are in the area of technology. While 35% of 18-year-olds with an autism spectrum diagnosis (ASD) attend college,[4] not all of them are interested in or qualified for technology-related roles. As a result, this creates a relatively small talent pool for technology jobs. Employers who think more broadly about the roles available for autistic employees will find a broader candidate pool.

Second, in seeking autistic candidates, many employers look to their traditional source for employees with disabilities: their local vocational services agency. Not everyone with autism, particularly college graduates, registers with their state vocational agency, as these organizations are not always effective in finding competitive employment for autistic candidates with college or advanced degrees. Employers also report mixed experiences with vocational rehabilitation (VR) agencies. A 2018 study completed by the US Government Accountability Office found that "(e)mployers in one of four discussion groups said that VR does not always provide enough qualified job candidates to meet their needs, and employers in another discussion group said that job candidates referred by VR are not always good matches for their hiring needs".[5] We will cover strategies for sourcing autistic talent in Chapter 8: Sourcing Autistic Jobseekers.

Launching Your Own Program

Based on our experience developing neurodiversity hiring programs for Fortune 1000 companies, we have identified four critical steps that are essential to successfully employing autistic professionals.

Build Buy-In

Every organization has a different process for making decisions and getting things done. Whether you work in an organization where decisions are driven from the top down or the bottom up, one thing is universally true: for decisions to get made, someone needs to drive them. Larry Smith, a defense strategist who held senior advisory positions in Congress and the Department of Defense, lists six reasons why organizations fail to execute their ideas. One of those reasons is "no battle captain" – to make an idea happen, appoint someone who has the clear responsibility and authority to make that idea happen.[6]

When launching a neurodiversity hiring program in your company, the role of "battle captain" comprises two major players working in tandem: sponsor and project leader. First, you need a "champion" or sponsor. Depending on how your organization makes decisions, that champion may be someone from the C-suite (i.e., CEO, CFO, COO, CIO, etc.), a leader of a division or business unit, or a champion of your company's current diversity and inclusion initiatives. Regardless of who the champion is, it is important for them to have the ability to influence your organization's diversity and inclusion and recruiting agendas and to direct the financial resources to support a program implementation.

A champion alone, however, is not the key to a successful program launch.[7] Appoint a project leader to focus on the program's day-to-day execution and coordinate the many people in the organization who will need to be involved to implement a successful neurodiversity hiring program. It is also critical to have broad-based outreach in your organization, creating awareness around program plans and seeking employees interested in being involved in the initiative. Enlist the help of those employees who have expressed their personal passion about autism: we find the most successful programs are those that engage employees who are volun*teers*, not volun*tolds*.

One of the most effective ways to build awareness, and buy-in, for a program is through events and training sessions targeted at employee resource groups (ERGs) and business resource groups (BRGs) focused on autism, disability, and/or diversity. Also, human resources, talent acquisition, and caregiver groups for employees with family members and friends connected to autism can be a good source for building support for a neurodiversity hiring initiative. All these groups include employees who are predisposed to and aligned with the objectives of such an effort.

Evaluate the Models

As discussed above, different models exist for how to attract and hire autistic employees into your workforce. Every organization has its own unique culture, and the different models available will work better for some organizations than others. It is important to consider a few factors when looking at the model you want to use to launch your program:

- What is the ultimate hiring goal for your organization? The number of individuals to be hired over what time period? Is the goal like SAP's – 1% of your workforce over time – or more modest?
- What is the skill level of the positions to be filled – professional versus non-professional hires? Do you expect the employees to work independently or are you willing to support employees with job coaches?
- Is the goal to have a program that is enterprise-wide or is the effort more targeted?
- If you create dedicated teams of autistic employees focusing on specific tasks, will your business flow be able to sustain their employment over time? If not, how will you create career paths for these employees?

- As your initiative grows, do different segments or geographies of your business require different models?

While it isn't necessary to have a firm answer to all these questions at the start of a pilot program, it is important to be thinking about these issues as you plan.

Consult the Experts

Understanding neurodiversity and autism is crucial in successfully attracting and retaining autistic employees. Unfortunately, the unemployment statistics for autistic college graduates confirm that our current systems for helping people with disabilities find employment isn't working for those with autism. With the greater understanding of the unemployment crisis in the autism community and the increasing number of employers focusing on autism hiring initiatives, organizations have emerged to help employers and autistic jobseekers come together. A listing of some of these organizations can be found in the *Autism@Work Playbook*,[8] which was created by SAP, Microsoft, JPMorgan Chase, EY, and the University of Washington.

Like the different program models mentioned earlier, these organizations vary in their approaches. When launching an autism hiring initiative, it is important to use experts who can provide your organization with knowledge about how to attract and retain autistic talent, as well as how to define and reach your ultimate program goals. Below are questions to consider when deciding which experts are the best fit for your organization:

- What is the background of the key staff regarding autism and neurodiversity? Do they have experience in and an appreciation for your work environment? Do they employ autistic talent on their own staff?
- What services will they be providing? Will they be subcontracting any of those services? If so, do you have approval over the choice of subcontractors?
- Do they represent you (the employer) or the jobseekers?
- If the organization offers a "temp to perm" or "extended training before job offer" model, what is the conversion rate of their candidates from temporary workers or trainees to permanent employees?
- How does the organization source candidates for you? What responsibility, if any, do you have for sourcing candidates? What is the retention rate of the candidates placed by the organization?
- Once candidates are on the job, what type of ongoing support and training do you (the employer) receive?

- Is there a required contract? If so, what are the contract terms to launch and grow an autism hiring program? Does the organization teach you how to run and grow your neurodiversity hiring program on your own over time?

Start Small

Everyone is familiar with the saying "Rome wasn't built in a day". When SAP announced the launch of their Autism at Work program in 2013, they gave themselves a seven-year time horizon to meet their hiring targets and they are still working toward that original goal.

If you are just beginning down this path, start with a pilot program. Generally starting with five to ten hires, a pilot program in one business division and/or location will allow for close control and monitoring over every aspect of the program. Use a pilot as a model to learn what works for your organization, what doesn't, and what you want to do differently next time. Perfect your pilot, then use it as a model to grow your program more broadly throughout your organization.

Conclusion

Standard recruiting and interviewing practices are a barrier to entry into the workforce for most autistic jobseekers. In 2013, SAP led the way in trying to combat this problem by establishing the first Autism@Work program targeted at hiring professional-level autistic individuals. Since then, over 50 other US corporations have launched or announced plans for similar programs.

Not every company implements the same model when establishing an autism hiring initiative. It is important to evaluate the available models to determine which will be the best fit for your organization. Building buy-in within your organization, appointing a champion and project leader, and consulting the experts will ensure you are ready to launch your pilot program.

Notes

1 Idaho Department of Vocational Rehabilitation. "About VR." September 1, 2020. https://vr.idaho.gov/about/.
2 US Department of Labor. "About WIOA." September 1, 2020. https://www.dol.gov/agencies/eta/wioa/about.
3 Bernick, Michael. "Effective Autism (Neurodiversity) Employment: A Legal Perspective." *Forbes*, September 1, 2020. https://www.forbes.com/sites/michaelbernick/2019/01/15/effective-autism-neurodiversity-employment-a-legal-perspective/.

4 Shattuck, Paul T., Sarah Carter Narendorf, Benjamin Cooper, Paul R. Sterzing, Mary Wagner, and Julie Lounds Taylor. "Postsecondary Education and Employment among Youth with an Autism Spectrum Disorder." *Pediatrics* 129, no. 6 (June 2012): 1042. https://doi.org/10.1542/peds.2011-2864.
5 GAO, US Government Accountability Office. "Vocational Rehabilitation: Additional Federal Information Could Help States Serve Employers and Find Jobs for People with Disabilities." *GAO-18-577*. Washington, DC. September 6, 2018. https://www.gao.gov/assets/700/694369.pdf.
6 Roberts, Paul. "The Art of Getting Things Done." *Fast Company*, May 31, 2000. https://www.fastcompany.com/39708/art-getting-things-done.
7 Ashkenas, Ron. "How to Be an Effective Executive Sponsor." *Harvard Business Review*, May 18, 2015. https://hbr.org/2015/05/how-to-be-an-effective-executive-sponsor.
8 Annabi, Hala, E. W. Crooks, Neil Barnett, J. Guadagno, James R. Mahoney, J. Michelle, A. Pacilio, Hiren Shukla, and Jose Velasco. *Autism @ Work Playbook: Finding Talent and Creating Meaningful Employment Opportunities for People with Autism*. Seattle, WA: ACCESS-IT, The Information School, University of Washington, 2019, 61.

Chapter 4

The Autistic Jobseeker
Not Your Typical Candidate

Job search sites such as Glassdoor, Monster, Indeed, and others all have "top lists" of what recruiters seek in interviewees. A review of these lists reveals some common themes. In addition to meeting role requirements, recruiters want to see candidates demonstrate the following behavioral characteristics in order to recommend them to a hiring manager:

- Strong communication skills
- A "can-do" or positive attitude
- Self-awareness
- Teamwork focus

Most recruiters are working on 30 to 40 open job requisitions at any time[1] and will interview four to six candidates[2] for each of those positions. A busy recruiter will interview thousands of people each year. Recruiters quickly develop a keen sense of what they are looking for in jobseekers during the interview process and how to screen out those who don't meet their requirements.

The behaviors recruiters typically rely on to evaluate candidates, however, may manifest differently in autistic individuals. The autistic brain processes information differently from that of a neurotypical individual or other neurodivergent individuals. Therefore, in an interview, autistic jobseekers may miss non-verbal cues, not anticipate the underlying meaning behind certain questions, or become distracted by noises. Additionally, individuals on the spectrum may experience more intense levels of anxiety than non-autistic candidates, exacerbating their primary challenges related to autism.

It is important to understand these differences and why autistic candidates may not present as expected. In this chapter, we will discuss how autistic jobseekers may not conform to recruiters' expectations as well as the role of social cognitive abilities, sensory sensitivities, and anxiety during the interview process. The discussions in this and the next chapter provide the foundational information for recruiters and hiring managers to better implement the strategies for recruiting, interviewing, and onboarding individuals on the spectrum.

> Not all autistic individuals will present the same. No two individuals on the spectrum are affected by autism the same way, and the behaviors they demonstrate related to autism will be unique to them.

The Unwritten Rules of the "Hidden Curriculum"

As will be discussed in Chapter 9, interviews are all about making a good impression. When meeting someone for the first time, we are dependent on our *social cognitive abilities* to send the right signals, pick up and interpret the signals being sent by the person we are meeting, and respond appropriately. Most jobseekers are familiar with the common "rules" of interviewing, which assume an understanding of what is called the *hidden curriculum*, the unspoken rules of behavior that allow us to "fit in" to any social situation in which we find ourselves. The hidden curriculum includes interpreting nonverbal communication such as gestures, body language, facial expressions, and tone of voice. These rules are considered "hidden" because they are based on information learned through observation and intuitive understanding, rather than explicit education. One such rule would be taking turns speaking in a meeting so as not to monopolize the conversation.

Job search sites, career coaches, and career services offices of colleges and universities all offer guidance to jobseekers on how to prepare for and conduct themselves in interviews. Unfortunately, much of the advice given creates a standard of performance for autistic candidates that is unachievable. Table 4.1 shows the differences between the expectations an interviewer may have of jobseekers vs. what they may observe in an autistic candidate.

Theory of Mind

Understanding the hidden curriculum allows one to know intuitively how to interpret and implement the interviewing rules listed in Table 4.1. During a job interview, an astute candidate reads the non-verbal messages an interviewer telegraphs through body language, tone of voice, or facial expressions and adjusts their behavior and responses accordingly. This ability – to understand what others are thinking without being told – is called *theory of mind*, or in layman's terms, "putting yourself in someone else's shoes".

Many autistic individuals struggle with theory of mind and understanding another's perspective. Consequently, they have difficulty with the unspoken rules of social situations (including interviews) as well as interpreting the reactions of others to their own behavior. For this reason, autistic individuals

Table 4.1 Interviewing Rules: Expected Responses vs. Autistic Candidates

Interviewing Rule	Expected Response	Autistic Candidate
Be aware of your body language, including dress, eye contact, posture, handshake, and smile.	Confirms dress code beforehand, has firm handshake, sits upright, maintains eye contact, smiles, telegraphs interest and enjoyment in the process through facial expressions and body language	May not dress appropriately or appears disheveled (i.e., shirt untucked), weak handshake, poor posture, avoids eye contact or stares, may have blank expression or inappropriate facial expressions, such as smiling at the wrong time
Discuss your successes/lessons learned.	When asked behavioral questions, uses the opportunity to highlight achievements and experience, explaining lessons learned from negative situations	When asked behavioral questions, may spend too much time describing the situation, not focus on their role in the outcome or any lessons learned, and talk about failures and negative experiences
Be positive.	Will use all opportunities to relate how they are a good fit for the role and their enthusiasm to be hired for the job in question	May struggle to highlight their strengths and revert to discussing their weaknesses and failures; may assume the recruiter knows they want the job by the fact they applied and not reinforce their enthusiasm for the role/employer
Keep answers concise and to the point.	Strives to address the key points of the question asked, will elaborate on questions that could be answered in one word	May provide too much information, not necessarily on topic, or give a one-word answer if the question is phrased to allow that
Ask thought-provoking questions.	Will have prepared questions and come up with relevant questions during the interview if the prepared questions have been addressed	May have prepared questions but struggle to develop additional questions during the interview if the prepared questions have been addressed

respond well to social rules that are unambiguous and require less subjective interpretation. Clear rules that define how an autistic candidate should behave in interviews (and on the job) also reduce the anxiety they may feel over misunderstanding another person's intentions. A further discussion of anxiety appears later in this chapter.

Theory of mind also plays a critical role in how we interpret the words of others. People often use figurative language such as metaphors, idioms, and sarcasm to say one thing while actually meaning or intending something else. For example, when making a sarcastic comment, the speaker's facial expression, tone of voice, and the context of the situation signal not to take what they are saying literally. Theory of mind helps the listener understand the intent of the remark. Some individuals on the spectrum tend towards *literal thinking* (discussed further in the next chapter). As a result, they often miss the intent of sarcasm, irony, and idioms, which causes them to misinterpret social interactions.

Although common interviewing rules are fraught with hidden curriculum and theory of mind challenges, these expectations can be revised for autistic candidates to provide clarity and specific guidance. Table 4.2 shows

Table 4.2 Autistic-Friendly Interviewing Rules

Original Interviewing Rule	Autistic-Friendly Interviewing Rule
Be aware of your body language, including dress, eye contact, posture, handshake, and smile.	• Confirm appropriate attire and visit the restroom beforehand to check your appearance • Sit in a straight-back chair if possible • If eye contact is a challenge, disclose that to the interviewer and focus on your answers (see Chapter 9 for interviewer guidance)
Discuss your successes/lessons learned.	When answering behavioral and/or situational questions, use the STAR method: • Describe the *Situation* • Explain the *Task* you had to perform • List the *Actions* you took • Describe the *Result*
Be positive.	Do not share negative stories or views of prior supervisors, colleagues, professors, or teammates. If asked to share a negative experience, describe the event briefly then explain either the lesson learned or what actions you took to improve your own abilities.
Keep answers concise and to the point.	If you are not sure how long an answer to give to a question: • Provide two to three sentences • Then ask the interviewer if they would like to hear more
Ask thought-provoking questions.	Research the company and bring written questions with you to every interview. If the interviewer answers your questions during the interview: • Write down other questions that may come up during the interview, which you can ask at the end • Take a moment to review your list of prepared questions, then indicate to the interviewer that they have all been answered

ways in which someone coaching an autistic individual might provide such guidance. A neurodivergent-friendly employer could also guide and support candidates by incorporating this information into their interviewing process.

These rewritten interviewing rules provide detailed guidance to give to autistic candidates on how to prepare for certain aspects of the interview, leaving little room for misinterpreting hidden curriculum issues or having to "read the mind" of the interviewer. For specific advice on rephrasing interview questions to minimize theory of mind challenges for autistic candidates, see Chapter 11.

Sensory Sensitivities

Most individuals, particularly when engaged in a task such as interviewing, have a sensory filter that allows them to block out distractions in their environment – hearing others talk, seeing people walk by, or smelling food being heated in a nearby pantry – so they can stay focused on the task at hand. For individuals on the spectrum, this filter may not exist, causing the individual to become distracted or experience *sensory overload*.

Sensory overload occurs when one or more of the five senses are overstimulated by the environment, providing more information than the brain can receive and process. Sensory overload can result in:

- Difficulty focusing due to competing sensory input
- Irritability
- Restlessness and discomfort
- Urge to cover one's ears or shield one's eyes from sensory input
- Feeling overly excited or "wound up"
- Stress, fear, or anxiety about one's surroundings[3]

Multiple studies have shown that individuals exposed to excessive levels of noise experience greater levels of anxiety, depression, and other physical ailments.[4] Some autistic candidates experience normal noise levels or everyday sights and smells more intensely, and the effects of this heightened response can be very disruptive to everyday activities. The conversation of others in the hallway may seem as loud to an autistic candidate as the one they are having with their interviewer, making it impossible to retain focus on the interview. The nearly imperceptible flickering of an overhead fluorescent light bulb may appear to someone on the spectrum as strong as the flashing of a disco ball. The overwhelming sensory bombardment felt by many autistic individuals is not only a distraction; it is a factor in increasing their overall level of anxiety.

Sensory sensitivities are one of the diagnostic criteria used to determine if someone is on the autism spectrum.[5] Keep in mind, however, that the degree to which someone experiences sensory sensitivities varies from person to person and is not something under their control. Chapter 9 discusses how to reduce the impact of sensory sensitivities when interviewing autistic candidates and Chapter 14 discusses how to create a workplace that allows employees with sensory sensitivities to avoid becoming overwhelmed. The goal is to create an environment that will minimize the risk of sensory overload for autistic candidates and colleagues.

Anxiety

The interview process for *any* job candidate can be nerve-wracking, but the challenges experienced by an autistic individual, whether related to the hidden curriculum or sensory sensitivities, can exacerbate this anxiety. Feeling anxious is not unique to autism: according to the National Institute of Mental Health, 19.1% of all US adults had an anxiety disorder during the past year, including panic disorder, generalized anxiety disorder, agoraphobia, specific phobia, social anxiety disorder, post-traumatic stress disorder, obsessive-compulsive disorder, and separation anxiety disorder.[6] However, up to 40% of those with an autism spectrum disorder diagnosis experience anxiety[7] and it is the most common co-occurring diagnosis for those with autism.[8] According to a 2019 survey of over 3,000 members of the UK technology community, incidences of anxiety and depression appeared much higher in the neurodivergent (84%) compared to the neurotypical (49%).[9]

Anxiety disorders can affect a person's ability to complete their daily living activities and impact their job performance. Many people on the autism spectrum experience this heightened anxiety as a normal part of their daily life, as explained by this autistic adult:

> Imagine you live in a world where everyone speaks a language you don't understand. Every day you know you are making social missteps and mistakes, because you don't speak the language and aren't able to learn it. You know everyone notices those mistakes and thinks the worst of you for them, but you don't know what to do about it.

At work, this "language" is largely based on non-verbal communication: facial expressions, body language, gestures, and tone of voice. Although researchers may debate exactly what percentage of our everyday communication is non-verbal, they all agree that the ability to decipher communication apart from spoken language is critical. In his book, *Emotions Revealed*, researcher Dr. Paul Ekman used his decades of research to explain how facial expressions provide clear signals about our emotions to those who can identify the clues.[10] It is estimated that the 40+ muscles in your face can form thousands of facial expressions, and the avoidance of eye contact that is typical of some people on the autism spectrum (see Chapter 9) makes these especially difficult to detect.

Conclusion

The behaviors recruiters typically rely on to evaluate candidates may manifest differently in autistic individuals, for whom reading social cues and decoding what other people might be thinking is a common struggle. The heavy reliance we have on non-verbal communication in general means that autistic people may misunderstand the intent of interviewers during the many interactions of the interview process. Those with sensory sensitivities will be tasked with managing in an environment filled with distractions.

The job search process is anxiety-producing for *any* individual; however, someone with autism has the additional burden of knowing they may miss important non-verbal cues or be hampered by sensory overload. This awareness can result in a vicious cycle of anxiety and failure, causing many autistic jobseekers to drop out of the process altogether. A significant portion of this book will focus on ways to eliminate the non-verbal communication and hidden curriculum messages, as well as the anxiety embedded in the recruiting, interviewing, and onboarding processes.

Notes

1 Maurer, Roy. "How Many Open Reqs Should In-House Recruiters Have?" *SHRM*, August 6, 2018. https://www.shrm.org/resourcesandtools/hr-topics/t alent-acquisition/pages/how-many-open-reqs-should-in-house-recruiters-have. aspx.
2 Turczynski, Bart. "2021 HR Statistics: Job Search, Hiring, Recruiting & Interviews." *Zety*, January 28, 2021. https://zety.com/blog/hr-statistics.
3 Watson, Kathryn. "Sensory Overload: Symptoms, Causes, Related Conditions, and More." *Healthline*, September 27, 2018. https://www.healthline.com/health/ sensory-overload.
4 Sheikh, Knvul. "Noise Pollution Isn't Just Annoying – It's Bad for Your Health." *Brainfacts.org*, June 27, 2018. https://www.brainfacts.org:443/thinking-sensing -and-behaving/diet-and-lifestyle/2018/noise-pollution-isnt-just-annoying-its-bad -for-your-health-062718.
5 CDC. "Diagnostic Criteria: Autism Spectrum Disorder (ASD)." *Centers for Disease Control and Prevention*, June 29, 2020. https://www.cdc.gov/ncbddd/ autism/hcp-dsm.html.
6 NIMH. "Statistics: Any Anxiety Disorder." *National Institute of Mental Health*, November 2017. https://www.nimh.nih.gov/health/statistics/any-anxiety-disor der.shtml.

7 Zaboski, Brian A., and Eric A. Storch. "Comorbid Autism Spectrum Disorder and Anxiety Disorders: A Brief Review." *Future Neurology* 13, no. 1 (February 2018): 31–37. https://doi.org/10.2217/fnl-2017-0030.

8 Burchi, Elisabetta, and Eric Hollander. "Anxiety in Autism Spectrum Disorder." *AADA*, March 26, 2018. https://adaa.org/learn-from-us/from-the-experts/blog -posts/consumer/anxiety-autism-spectrum-disorder.

9 BIMA. "The Voices of Our Industry: BIMA Tech Inclusion & Diversity Report 2019." *BIMA*, 2019. https://bima.co.uk/wp-content/uploads/2020/01/BIMA -Tech-Inclusion-and-Diversity-Report-2019.pdf, 25.

10 Ekman, Paul. *Emotions Revealed: Recognizing Faces and Feelings to Improve Communication and Emotional Life.* New York: Henry Holt, 2007.

Chapter 5

Differences in Autistic Thinking

Our brains are composed of billions of nerve cells, called neurons, which communicate with each other across their various regions using electromechanical signals.[1] Although it is common to hear the phrase "the autistic brain is wired differently", the neurobiology of autistic brains is an evolving field, so there is no definitive answer as to how they differ from those of neurotypicals. Some research suggests that autistic brains have areas of over-connectivity and under-connectivity that may cause individuals with autism to struggle with tasks that require combining or assimilating information that resides in different parts of the brain, like social interaction and communication. Yet when required to do a specific task primarily focused within a single brain region, such as paying attention to details, individuals with autism may excel in comparison to their neurotypical peers.[2]

No one thinks exactly like someone else. Researchers have demonstrated that people, in general, show individual differences in *cognitive styles,* the habitual ways we process information for tasks involving decision-making, problem-solving, perception, and attention. Neurodivergent people process information in ways that vary significantly from neurotypicals, and these differences are more pronounced in certain areas.

For example, someone on the autism spectrum may become so absorbed in the details of a project that they work late into the night – not noticing that their teammates have all gone home for the day. On the flip side, the same individual may struggle starting a new assignment, while the rest of their team is waiting for their work. Both situations demonstrate "out-of-sync" *executive functioning skills* – those cognitive skills that allow us to put our knowledge and intelligence to work to accomplish a task.

These differences in thought processes can result in difficulties for autistic individuals around "seeing the big picture", understanding context, learning from experience, thinking intuitively, and working efficiently. On the other hand, an autistic individual's way of thinking that may cause a problem in one area may be quite beneficial in another.

Although an in-depth coverage of the thought processes associated with autism is beyond the scope of this book, this chapter will provide recruiters and interviewers an understanding of the various challenges and strengths related to how autistic people process information. It serves as the basis for many of the suggestions and accommodations for interviewing and onboarding that appear in later chapters.

Not all autistic individuals will present the same. No two individuals on the spectrum are affected by autism the same way, and the behaviors they demonstrate related to autism will be unique to them.

Disorder, Disability, or Difference?

As you learn about autism, you may find it referred to interchangeably as a "developmental disorder", an "invisible disability", or a "brain difference". Although related, these terms are quite different from each other and can affect how neurodivergent conditions are perceived.

Based on the "medical model", autism spectrum disorder (ASD) is categorized as a *neurodevelopmental disorder,* according to the *Diagnostic and Statistical Manual of Mental Disorders* (DSM), the reference used by clinicians and researchers to assess and classify mental disorders. It is important to distinguish between a developmental disorder, such as autism, and *psychiatric disorders*. One of the most important aspects one must understand about ASD is that it is not a mental illness. It is a developmental disorder and lifelong cognitively-based condition that affects social interactions and whose challenges may vary according to life stage and circumstances. Psyciatric disorders (e.g.depression), on the other hand, are emotional, not cognitively-based, and may change over time. The DSM is used primarily for diagnosis, and as such does not include information or guidelines for treatment for any of the disorders it lists. It also does not differentiate among the variety of impacts those with an ASD diagnosis may experience related to being autistic. Anyone meeting the diagnostic criteria will be given an autism spectrum disorder diagnosis.

Disability is a legal term that the Americans with Disabilities Act of 1990 (ADA) uses to determine eligibility for accommodations in the workplace. According to the ADA, a person with a disability has a mental or physical problem that interferes with major life activities such as performing tasks at work or engaging in social interactions. Invisible disabilities, such as autism, bipolar disorder, multiple sclerosis, diabetes, and epilepsy, to name a few, are not always obvious, so employers can request medical documentation (such as a DSM diagnosis for autism) showing that the employee needs special accommodations.

In contrast, a brain *difference* refers to the natural variation in styles of thinking. Differences are less marked in people who are considered "average" on a given cognitive trait and are neither good nor bad per se. However, as differences veer further from the norm, they may cause difficulties and require accommodations to create a fit between the person and environment in which they work. More extreme differences may also be associated with a unique strength or ability in the person that is valued in the workplace.

It is difficult for neurotypicals to understand the thinking style of someone whose brain is "wired differently", so the natural tendency is to try to make neurodivergent thinking conform to ours – usually with little success. It is interesting to note that just as autistic individuals who struggle with theory of mind cannot understand how neurotypicals think, it can be equally difficult for neurotypicals to understand the thinking style of someone on the spectrum. Even among neurotypicals, we often struggle with theory of mind in understanding the experiences of those who differ from us by race, nationality, gender identity, sexual orientation, and religion. According to psychologist Thomas Armstrong:

> We shouldn't focus all of our attention on making a neurodiverse person adapt to the environment in which they find themselves, which is a little like making a round peg fit in a square hole. We should also devise ways of helping an individual change their surrounding environment to fit the needs of their unique brain.[3]

Changing the environment starts with recruiters, interviewers, and hiring managers reframing their thinking about autism and other neurodivergent conditions, and understanding the ways in which the thinking of neurodivergent individuals differs from their own rather than focusing on them as mental disorders or disabilities. The next sections will focus on the challenges and strengths related to differences in various cognitive styles and thinking processes of people on the autism spectrum.

Seeing the "Big Picture"

A person's *cognitive style* reflects their typical way of thinking, remembering, and solving problems. One of the cognitive styles in which autistic people may differ the most is *central coherence*, the tendency to pull information from multiple sources into a unified whole or "big picture".

Central Coherence

Central coherence is an effective way of processing information, allowing us to get the gist of something without needing all the specifics. Working from the "top down", we fill in details when necessary to fit the larger mental picture. Everyone is somewhere on the central coherence continuum, and people with strong central coherence can intuitively grasp a main idea without needing to pay close attention to the details. Research suggests that some people with autism have *weak central coherence*,[4] so they tend to process details from the "bottom up", typically thinking about things in the smallest possible parts. They may be able to recall exact details yet miss the overall meaning.

In the business world, people who excel at big picture thinking and envisioning broad goals are referred to as "strategic thinkers" or "visionaries", while "tactical thinkers" excel at implementing the details that make the plan work. Most people have aspects of each type of thinking and can shift focus between the big picture and the details to accomplish a goal. Keep in mind that weak central coherence is not a deficit; rather it reflects a bias toward detail-oriented thinking.

Weak central coherence is also associated with strengths, such as performing repetitive tasks where accuracy, rules, and routine are important. The ability to notice small details of a pattern, theory, object, or visual image is also associated with a higher degree of *systematizing* – the drive to analyze or construct systems by noting regularities, structure, and rules to predict how the system will behave. Systems are part of every facet of the world, from math and mechanics to weather patterns, musical notation, and patterns in sports performance (as portrayed in the movie *Moneyball*). In his book *The Pattern Seekers: How Autism Drives Human Invention*, psychologist and autism researcher Simon Baron-Cohen argues that while not every inventor is autistic and not all autistic people are inventors, inventors and autistic people share similar minds. These "hyper-systemizers" often have difficulty navigating the complexities of the social world, but they can excel in any field in which they can search for "if-and-then" patterns (*if* x happens *and* y happens, *then* z will happen) to analyze systems or create new ones.[5] According to an autistic professional:

> I think one of the great skills we possess is the ability to observe things in a way that says, "That's really smart, that's great technology, this works fantastic" or "That's really flawed" – there are ten things you can remove from there and still be just as effective without wasting so much time.

Although it may not be automatic or intuitive, people on the spectrum *can* process information for overall meaning, especially if prompted to do so. Providing the context of a situation to an individual who struggles with central coherence will help them see the "big picture".

Context

Central coherence is related to *context*, the lens through which one views a situation or circumstance. It encompasses the ability to set priorities, learn from a previous situation that is like a current one, or act appropriately in social situations. An individual on the autism spectrum often has difficulty "connecting the dots", i.e., processing facts and bits of information within context. According to Dr. Peter Vermeulen, an expert in the field of autism, people on the spectrum are "context blind": they may be aware of the context but not able to apply or use it spontaneously.[6]

Context-blindness explains why it may be difficult for autistic people to process ambiguous information, especially in social situations, and adjust their behavior accordingly. For example, what may seem like an obvious question to an interviewer, "Tell me about yourself", can be confusing to an autistic candidate:

> I think the question that makes me the most uncomfortable is the first one, "Tell us a little bit about yourself". I never know quite where to begin ... Do you want to know my favorite color? Do you want to know where I've been the last five years? Do you want to know about my education, about my family? All these different things are going through my head because I don't really know what you want.

Neurotypical jobseekers intuitively know that the context of the interview requires answering this question by focusing on their skill sets and related experience, but this is not obvious to all autistic individuals. Framing interview questions to include context makes them less ambiguous and helps to alleviate anxiety.

Since they may not rely on context to process details, people with autism often make more consistent decisions and have a fresh perspective on solving a problem or doing an analysis, as they are less apt to be influenced by office politics, assumptions, or the status quo. Many autistic individuals have come up with new and creative ways of solving problems because they do not adhere to conventional ways of doing things.

Literal Thinking

Our daily conversations are filled with shortcuts, idioms, metaphors, and figurative language. Understanding social communication involves assessing what the message is about, rather than focusing on what it *literally* says. Central coherence plays a large part, and for neurotypicals this is intuitive. They use theory of mind and context to understand the situation (the "big picture") and incorporate the literal meaning of the words spoken (the details) to interpret the intended meaning.

Many people on the autism spectrum are *literal thinkers*, who take the written and spoken word at face value and do not automatically understand what was implied. This is one of the biggest challenges for autistic talent throughout the recruiting, interviewing, and onboarding process, so use precise language and avoid idioms, metaphors, acronyms, and figurative speech when:

- Writing job descriptions (see Chapter 7)
- Asking interview questions (see Chapter 11)
- Making job offers and describing the onboarding process (see Chapter 12)

Literal thinkers also tend to view the world in terms of "black and white" or "right and wrong". They consider information, procedures, and their own observations as "fact" and may rigidly insist that these are not subject to interpretation. However, autistic individuals are usually very good at following rules, sequences, and tasks that require strict adherence to procedure, compliance, and codes, so with the right structure they can be very efficient and valuable assets in the workplace.

Keep in mind that these cognitive processes are all components of the "bigger picture" that enables us to make sense of the world and function within it, as illustrated in Figure 5.1.

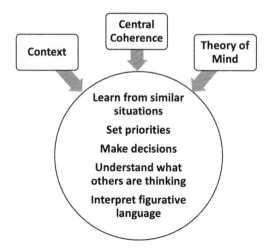

Figure 5.1 Components of the "Bigger Picture".

Reasoning and Decision-Making

> "Nowhere am I so desperately needed as on a shipload of illogical humans".[7]
>
> – Mr. Spock

Neurotypical brains are wired for efficiency so that tasks and everyday decisions do not need much deliberation. Using prior knowledge, experience, and intuition to make assumptions and "fill in the blanks" allows the transfer of knowledge from one situation to another without the need to "start from scratch".

Most people on the autism spectrum, however, are logical thinkers whose brains are wired for accuracy over speed. They approach decision-making and problem-solving by relying on detailed information and deliberation and have a low tolerance for ambiguity. These differences can make "thinking on the spot" and completing tasks in a timely manner challenging.

Transfer of Learning and Making Inferences

The brain will always look for similarities in details and between situations. Transfer of learning, or *generalization*, happens when you focus on the features that are similar in two situations rather than what is unique to each one. Without generalization, you would need to start at "square one" for every task because even minor differences would make each task appear different. Finding past solutions based on experience and using them as a template when working on something new that is related saves a great deal of time and energy in the workplace and in life in general.

Individuals on the spectrum often use precise information and are highly attuned to changes in their environment, including minor differences that might seem insignificant to others. Because of their detail-oriented cognitive style, they can have challenges with generalization, as they are more likely to focus on what is different than see a similarity between something they have done before and what they currently need to do. However, psychologist Simon Baron-Cohen considers this inability to generalize a benefit to those who are hyper-systemizers (as discussed previously) and explains, "A good systemizer is a splitter, not a lumper, since lumping things together can lead to missing key differences that enable you to predict how these two things behave differently".[8]

In social interactions, difficulty with generalization may prevent an autistic individual from applying the appropriate hidden curriculum rule, as no two social situations are exactly alike. On the job, employees who struggle with generalizing may take longer to apply the approach used for one task to another task that is similar, but can do so if provided clear guidance and instructions.

Another efficient brain process involves reasoning based on *inference* – a conclusion or "educated guess" that is not explicitly stated but is drawn from current evidence and past experience. Making inferences is a part of daily life and depends on the ability to integrate world knowledge within a specific context or situation: if you see someone carrying an umbrella, you might infer that it is going to rain. Job hunting involves making inferences about what recruiters and interviewers might be looking for in one's background and experience, which is particularly challenging for autistic individuals with theory of mind challenges.[9]

Deliberation vs. Intuition

We do not always make decisions the same way every time. Everyday decisions are often based on *intuition* or a "gut feeling", and social communication, in general, depends on intuitive cognitive processing that is quick, automatic, and effortless. More important decisions often involve *deliberation*, long and careful consideration that requires more time and information. While most of us switch between these two ways of thinking without much effort, autistic individuals typically have a reasoning style that is more circumspect, requiring more data before making a decision. Researchers suggest that this cognitive style involves higher deliberative and lower intuitive processing than in the general population but does not necessarily reflect a deficit in intuitive thinking per se.[10] See Chapter 11 for a further discussion of deliberative thinking.

One consequence of relying on a more deliberative style of reasoning is that individuals on the spectrum may have greater difficulty with a variety of everyday decisions, "over-thinking" minor decisions such as what to wear to work. However, they show no difference from neurotypicals in the ability to make unique and highly important life decisions, where deliberative thinking might be more effective.

As deliberative thinkers, individuals with autism are less likely to "jump to conclusions" and make decisions without sufficient evidence. They may appear to process information more slowly, as they consider all available information before coming to a conclusion. Greater deliberation also means that the thinking of autistic people is usually less biased or influenced by context than that of neurotypicals. For example, when asked "if a bat and a ball cost 1 dollar and 10 cents and the bat costs 1 dollar more than the ball, how much does the ball cost?" adults with autism are less likely to give the typical – yet incorrect – intuitive answer that the ball costs 10 cents.[11,12]

Executive Functioning

The higher-level cognitive processes that allow us to use our intelligence and knowledge effectively are called *executive functioning skills* (see Table 5.1[13]). Individuals with executive functioning challenges are often mistakenly judged as lacking in intelligence, skill sets, or motivation. This is not the case. In the job search process, executive functioning skills are key in keeping an individual on track in finding and pursuing appropriate employment opportunities.

Table 5.1 Executive Functioning Skills

Plan	Manage Time
• Organize thoughts and materials • Prioritize	• Estimate and allocate time needed • Get started • Adjust processing speeds
Focus	**Working Memory**
• Follow through and complete tasks • Avoid distractions and shift attention	• Remember details • Draw on past learning
Remain Flexible	**Regulate Emotions**
• Transition between tasks • Cope with changes in routine	• Manage frustration and emotions • Think before speaking

Those with autism, ADD, ADHD, non-verbal learning disabilities, mental health issues, and other social cognitive challenges may struggle in certain areas of executive functioning or process information in a non-typical fashion. Challenges related to executive functioning can be an obstacle to jobseekers in planning, initiating, and managing their job search, but may not be as obvious to recruiters and hiring managers during an interview. Executive functioning challenges may show up in an interview when candidates are required to switch quickly to a new topic of conversation or answer multipart questions. It can also be difficult for autistic individuals to apply rules without an explicit indication of how they are to be applied, detect when the rules have changed, or handle exceptions to a rule.[14] Executive functioning challenges may contribute to autistic jobseekers taking significantly longer than their neurotypical peers to find appropriate employment.

Many of these issues, if they exist, are more likely to present on the job (see Chapter 15 for a discussion of performance issues). However, understanding how the autistic brain is "wired" and how that impacts an individual's executive functioning capabilities is critical to providing a successful interview experience.

The Importance of Previewing

As you have seen throughout this chapter, autistic jobseekers may exhibit atypical patterns of cognitive performance, demonstrating strengths in certain styles of cognitive thinking, yet displaying challenges in others. For example, an autistic candidate may have a photographic recall of all the data in a multi-page report but be unable to remember dates from their resume.[15] In an interview environment, differences related to processing may appear as someone who takes an extra beat of time before answering questions, provides too much technical detail, or spends too much time answering one question, leaving the interviewer with insufficient time to ask their remaining questions.

Autistic interviewees faced with questions with which they are unfamiliar may need more time to formulate answers, forget the question, or digress. On the other hand, when asked questions with which they are familiar or in their area of expertise, they may provide overly in-depth, extensive responses. A person's ability to process information can be affected by several factors. The most obvious impact on a candidate's processing ability is their anxiety level.

One way to minimize a candidate's anxiety is through *previewing*, the guidance given in advance of an interview to autistic candidates so they know what the interviewer wants and expects. Previewing helps candidates manage their responses more effectively and maintain their focus on what you would like to know about them. This includes:

- Who they will be meeting with (provide a photo)
- How long to expect the entire interview will take
- What types of questions will be asked
- How much detail you expect
- How long an answer you expect

The job search and interviewing process is complex and requires the ability to receive and comprehend large amounts of information in multiple formats. Not only is previewing instrumental in helping autistic jobseekers prepare for and succeed in interviews (see Chapter 10), it helps throughout the entire onboarding process as well.

Autistic individuals often struggle to assimilate the many written, spoken, and non-verbal messages they receive from job descriptions and interviewers during their job search. Providing the following, with enough time for the individual to process and incorporate the information, will increase interviewing competency and reduce anxiety:

- Clearly written job descriptions, with no acronyms, jargon, idioms, or metaphors that delineate required skill sets from "nice to have" requirements (see Chapter 7)
- Interview guidelines, including instructions on the appropriate attire, the names and titles of interviewers, and the interview schedule with the times and locations of each meeting
- A suggested list of interview questions for preparation
- A contact person for questions

Conclusion

In his groundbreaking book, *NeuroTribes*, award-winning science journalist Steve Silberman chronicled autism from the historical, scientific, and social perspective, advocating for a more humane world in which people with neurological differences have access to the resources they need to live happier and more meaningful lives.[16] Indeed, the aim of the neurodiversity move-ment is to support neurodivergent people so they can contribute to society as they *are*, rather than how society dictates. This requires that those who are *not* neurodivergent understand the differences in how individuals with autism think, acknowledging their difficulties and providing support while recognizing and appreciating their strengths. Managers of autistic employ-ees who take this approach report becoming better managers of *all* their employees.

The challenges people on the autism spectrum may have with seeing the big picture, understanding context, thinking literally, generalizing, and thinking intuitively can be offset by abilities to detect and remember things that others may overlook, identify and create systems of all types, demon-strate new and creative ways to solve problems, and think things through without jumping to conclusions. The rest of this book will help recruiters and interviewers expand their awareness of how these brain differences relate to recruiting, interviewing, and onboarding autistic candidates.

Notes

1 Weaver II, Elizabeth A., and Hilary H. Doyle. "How Does the Brain Work?" *Dana Foundation* (blog), August 11, 2019. https://www.dana.org/article/how-do es-the-brain-work/.
2 Rossi, Carey. "Autism Spectrum Disorder: Autistic Brains vs Non-Autistic Brains." *Psycom.Net* (blog), May 4, 2020. https://www.psycom.net/autism-brain -differences.
3 Armstrong, Thomas. "Neurodiversity: A Concept Whose Time Has Come." *Institute4Learning*, February 14, 2021. https://www.institute4learning.com/ resources/articles/neurodiversity/.
4 Happé, Francesca, and Uta Frith. "The Weak Coherence Account: Detail-Focused Cognitive Style in Autism Spectrum Disorders." *Journal of Autism and Developmental Disorders* 36, no. 1 (2006): 5–25. https://doi.org/10.1007/ s10803-005-0039-0.
5 Baron-Cohen, Simon. *The Pattern Seekers: How Autism Drives Human Invention*. New York: Basic Books, 2020.
6 Vermeulen, Peter. *Autism as Context Blindness*. Shawnee Mission, KS: AAPC Publishing, 2012.
7 Poem of Quotes. "I, Mudd Quotes." March 10, 2021. https://www.poemofqu otes.com/quotes/film-tv/i-mudd-quotes.
8 Baron-Cohen, Simon. "Theories of the Autistic Mind." *The Psychologist* 21, no. 2 (2008): 112–116.
9 Bodner, Kimberly E., Christopher R. Engelhardt, Nancy J. Minshew, and Diane L. Williams. "Making Inferences: Comprehension of Physical Causality, Intentionality, and Emotions in Discourse by High-Functioning Older Children, Adolescents, and Adults with Autism." *Journal of Autism and Developmental Disorders* 45, no. 9 (September 2015): 2721–2733. https://doi.org/10.1007/s 10803-015-2436-3.
10 Morsanyi, Kinga, and Ruth M. J. Byrne, eds. *Thinking, Reasoning, and Decision Making in Autism*. London: Routledge, 2020.

11 The correct answer is 5 cents: if the bat costs $1.00 more than the ball and the total is $1.10, then the ball must cost 5 cents and the bat must cost $1.05. Most people read it as though the bat costs a definitive $1.00, but if the ball were to cost ten cents then both together would cost $1.20.

12 Morsanyi, *Thinking, Reasoning, and Decision Making in Autism.*

13 Scheiner, Marcia, and Joan Bogden. *An Employer's Guide to Managing Professionals on the Autism Spectrum.* London: Jessica Kingsley Publishers, 2017, 122.

14 Stuurman, S., H. J. M. Passier, Frédérieke Geven, and E. Barendsen. "Autism: Implications for Inclusive Education with Respect to Software Engineering." In CSERC '19: Proceedings of the 8th Computer Science Education Research Conference, Larnaca, Cyprus, 2019, 15–25. New York: Association for Computing Machinery (ACM). https://doi.org/10.1145/3375258.3375261.

15 Haigh, Sarah M., Jennifer A. Walsh, Carla A. Mazefsky, Nancy J. Minshew, and Shaun M. Eack. "Processing Speed Is Impaired in Adults with Autism Spectrum Disorder, and Relates to Social Communication Abilities." *Journal of Autism and Developmental Disorders* 48, no. 8 (August 1, 2018): 2653–2662. https://doi.org/10.1007/s10803-018-3515-z.

16 Silberman, Steve. *NeuroTribes: The Legacy of Autism and the Future of Neurodiversity.* New York, NY: Avery, 2016.

Part II

Recruiting Autistic Talent

Chapter 6

Screening Techniques for the Atypical Resume

Autistic jobseekers present differently from neurotypical candidates, both on paper and in person. As a result of their struggles with social communication, many autistic individuals will have spotty or non-existent professional experience when compared to their non-autistic peers. They may also struggle to articulate, or even understand, how their educational experiences, skill sets, and interests can translate into valuable workplace skills, leaving the hiring organization guessing as to which roles would be most appropriate for the candidate. When determining the best job fit for each candidate, it is necessary to assess the underlying skill sets of autistic candidates first and then match those with the requirements of your specific hiring needs.

> Keep in mind that just as with neurotypical candidates, it is important not to assume that all autistic candidates are the same in their skill sets, talents, capabilities, and challenges related to autism.

Appropriate roles exist for neurodivergent candidates across all business functions and levels. This chapter explores finding the right "job fit" for autistic individuals and assessing skills-based or functional resumes to reveal competencies, potential, and demonstrated effort.

Job Fit

As recruiters of autistic talent for employers, we are often asked "What are the best jobs for someone with autism?" Although our first inclination is to say "inclusive, competitive jobs", we don't want to appear flippant or rude. This question is well-intentioned, as it's based on the popular misconception that most autistic people excel in technology and computer science. However, the correct answer *is* "inclusive, competitive jobs". As with any individual, autistic individuals have skill sets and learning styles that can fit with many of the jobs any employer needs to fill; each employee, autistic or not, will be different.

While no one job category or classification is "ideal" for someone on the spectrum, autistic candidates may demonstrate strengths in certain areas of performance. Autistic talent can excel in key areas requiring:

- Attention to detail and accuracy
- Depth of knowledge/subject matter expertise
- Pattern recognition/error perception
- Intense focus on repetitive or routine tasks
- Creative, or non-apparent, solutions to problems

However, the features of the role itself and the nature of the work environment are also key factors in how successfully an autistic employee adapts to a job, as listed in Table 6.1.

Table 6.1 Features of Jobs and Work Environments for Autistic Employees

Desirable	*Potentially Difficult*
Structured	Chaotic/frenetic
Predictable	Noisy
Well-defined	Unpredictable
Knowledge-based	Sales-oriented
Task-oriented	High-stress customer service
Individual contributor	

Ultimately, when determining job fit, the critical question to ask is *"Is the job and work environment structured in such a way to ensure success for a neurodivergent candidate?"* If the answer is yes, then an autistic individual exists who is able to fill that job. That is not to say that any autistic individual will be able to fill all jobs in your organization, but keep in mind, this is true for neurotypical candidates as well.

The Myth of the Computer Geek

In 1944, when Hans Asperger published his first description of what he called "autistic psychopathy" in children, he referred to them as "little professors": boys who often had an intense interest in a narrow topic and would lecture on that topic in extreme detail but struggled with reciprocal conversation. From the "little professor" moniker sprang the myth of the savant and/or math whiz – think Dustin Hoffman's character in *Rain Man*, or Sheldon from *The Big Bang Theory* – as the embodiment of an autistic individual with exceptional intellectual capabilities.

Unfortunately, these stereotypes continue to do a disservice to the autistic community in their search for employment. Dr. Stephen Shore, a college professor and well-known autism advocate, is often quoted for saying, "If you've met one person with autism, you've met one person with autism".[1] Not only is this true in how individuals with an autism spectrum diagnosis are impacted by autism, it is also reflected in their breadth of skill sets, career interests, and professional goals.

At Integrate Autism Employment Advisors, we run a networking program for autistic college students and college graduates. Of the over 300 individuals who have attended this program, the majors/career interests of the program participants are as follows:

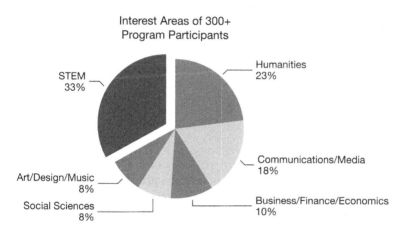

Interest Areas of 300+
Program Participants

STEM 33%

Humanities 23%

Communications/Media 18%

Business/Finance/Economics 10%

Social Sciences 8%

Art/Design/Music 8%

Figure 6.1 Interest Areas of Autistic College Students and Graduates in the Integrate Program.

The individuals who have found jobs after attending this program include:

Physician	Graphic Designer	Marketing Analyst
Environmental Engineer	Media Associate	Quantitative Analyst
Paralegal	Production Assistant	Software Engineer
Accountant	Archivist	Software Developer
Actuary	Translator/Linguist	Bioinformatics Engineer

Autistic individuals can thrive as artists, writers, lobbyists, lawyers, librarians, research scientists, architects, editors, journalists, and the list goes on.

Pigeonholing autistic candidates into specific job categories will limit your organization's access to the depth of this available talent pool.

The Atypical Resume

Recruiters are busy people. Data gathered from websites such as Glassdoor and The Ladders shows that recruiters receive on average 250 resumes for every job posting and spend six seconds scanning a resume.[2] If a resume is getting only six seconds of someone's attention, and it has to compete with 249 other resumes, it better stand out in the crowd. Additionally, an experienced recruiter also scans for "red flags", such as unexplained employment gaps and excessive job-hopping, which may create doubt in a recruiter's mind about a candidate's ability to do the job. Anytime a recruiter has a concern about a candidate based on the resume review, it is only natural to expect that they will pass on that candidate and move on to one of the many other submitted resumes.

Recruiters and hiring managers at mid- to large-sized companies (including an estimated 98.8% of the Fortune 500[3]) generally use an applicant tracking system (ATS) to automatically sort, filter, or rank candidates. A resume that doesn't contain the right search terms for work experience and skill sets can potentially eliminate an applicant, even if that candidate is highly qualified for the job.

Reviewing a Standard Resume

Typically, whether a resume is reviewed manually or automatically, relevant work history is often the first consideration in the process; if job experience is unrelated to the role or contains the red flags mentioned earlier, the candidate is most likely rejected. A standard resume review is mainly a "vertical" process of elimination, as depicted in Figure 6.2.

Reviewing an Atypical Resume

Unfortunately for autistic candidates, the resume review is the first roadblock they hit in the interview process. Because they have struggled to obtain employment in their field of choice, or focused all their energies on completing college (typically with a strong GPA), the resumes of autistic candidates oftentimes do not appear as competitive as those of their neurotypical peers – possibly lacking in internships, volunteer activities, and extracurriculars. Furthermore, successfully getting a resume through a screening process involves customizing for key terms and attributes that reflect the job description – "reading the mind" of the recruiter or ATS. An individual who struggles with *theory of mind* (see Chapter 4) may have difficulty presenting their experience and skill sets in a way that answers the specific needs of the person evaluating their resume.

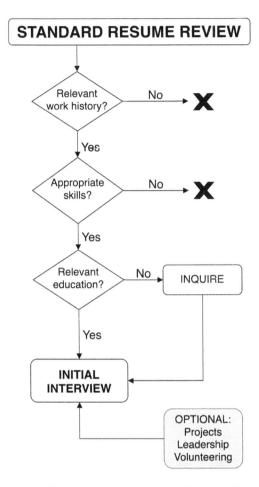

Figure 6.2 Standard Resume "Vertical" Review Process.

Some employers provide neurodivergent candidates an option to self-identify to a recruiter or someone involved in an Autism@Work hiring effort when they are applying through the company's career portal. Consequently, that candidate's resume will also be screened by someone familiar with neurodiversity. This manual intervention into an automated process allows for the autism-friendly review process discussed below to occur more frequently.

When recruiting autistic individuals, it is important to review resumes with an eye for skill sets and talents that may be demonstrated through non-traditional means. While the standard resume review is mainly a vertical process, reviewing an autistic candidate's resume is a more "horizontal"

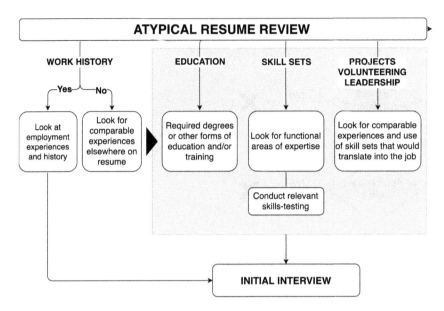

Figure 6.3 "Horizontal" Review Process for the Atypical Resume.

process that involves looking at the relationship between education, functional areas of expertise, comparable experiences, and use of skill sets that would translate into the job (see Figure 6.3).

Work History

For the remainder of this chapter we will discuss the atypical resume review process by analyzing the resumes of three autistic candidates: one who is currently working outside of their desired field, one who has no paid work experience, and a third who has had multiple work experiences but not been able to maintain steady employment.

Unrelated Work History

Many neurodivergent individuals will work at jobs outside their field of choice, often underemployed, while they continue to seek their first competitive, professional position. Others may have had difficulty getting that first paid job, despite having the required education and skill sets, for the many reasons discussed throughout this book.

Candidate 1 graduated in 2012 with a B.S. in Computer Science, Technological Systems Management, with a professional goal of becoming a software developer. By 2014 he had not found a job in that field, so he accepted a position as a Pharmacy Technician for a chain drug store and spent five years working there. In 2019, Integrate recruited him for a job as a Software Developer with a global insurance company, as part of their neurodiversity hiring initiative. The first part of his resume is shown below:

Candidate 1 (Software Developer)

Education

Rochester Institute of Technology	Rochester, NY
Bachelor of Science – GPA 3.2	May 2012
Majors: Computer Science, Technological Systems Management	

Experience

Rite Aid Pharmacy	Buffalo, NY
Pharmacy Technician	Aug. 2014–Present

- Input data for over 100 prescriptions daily, and maintain inventory
- Verify that patient information is up to date, accurate, and HIPPA compliant
- Provide customer service by setting up automated reminders for medications

Rochester Institute of Technology	Rochester, NY
Teaching Assistant, Computer Science Department	Aug.–Dec. 2012

- Provided students complementary lab sessions twice a week and extra test preparation
- Demonstrated Java and object-oriented programming concepts

If this were the resume of a typical applicant applying for a Software Developer role, his unrelated work experience as a Pharmacy Technician would raise a red flag – after all, most likely the majority of candidates seven years out of school with a degree in computer science have had at least some work experience in that field. However, when viewed through the lens of the atypical resume review process pictured above, a different picture emerges.

First, his five-year work history demonstrates the ability to hold a job that requires data management. It also shows a desire to be productively employed, even if the job is below his skill level. The Computer Skills section on the next page shows that he has extensive knowledge of programming languages and the skills necessary for developing applications and websites.

Second, whereas personal projects and interests would generally not be a major factor when evaluating a typical resume, for autistic candidates they can offer comparable experiences or skill sets that would translate into the job. In his Personal Projects section on the next page, *Candidate 1* shows how he has kept current with the necessary programming languages and technologies while continuing to look for a job as a Software Developer:

Candidate 1 (Software Developer)

Computer Skills
Programming Languages: Java, Python, JavaScript, Objective C, Ruby
Web: HTML, CSS
IDEs: Eclipse, XCode, Sublime
Other: XML, SQL, Bash, LaTex, Windows 10, OSX
Personal Projects
Game Development
- Fantasy Toolbox: Created tools and RSS feed to facilitate managing teams using Python and Yahoo Fantasy Sports API
- Game of Life: Created a version of Conway's *Game of Life*, a cellular automation, for iOS using Objective C
Programming Competition
- Created *Emojifi* for Video HackDay 2017 Hackathon
- Employed jquery, node.js, and Clarafai API to overlay video with relevant emoji on any given frame

---

Overall, while this jobseeker did not have work experience in the software development field seven years after graduating from college, he was able to demonstrate his ability to maintain a good employment record, how he kept his technical skills current, and the perseverance of not giving up on his ultimate career goal.

No Paid Work History

Many autistic jobseekers will not have any job experience on their resumes. For many neurodivergent college students, their focus on completing school-work takes precedence over all else, and they often miss the opportunities for internships or paid work. Additionally, some autistic college students will carry a reduced course load and take courses during the summer semester to complete their degrees. Lastly, a number of autistic individuals just struggle to find work and remain unemployed, despite their best efforts to find any type of employment. Once again, for these candidates, focusing on their skill sets and capabilities is key in reviewing their resumes to determine if they should be considered for a position.

Because a standard resume review process is so quick (either automatically by ATS or through skillful skimming), it relies on a process of elimination until a few candidates emerge with all boxes checked. In contrast, an atypical resume review process relies on inclusion rather than exclusion; the recruiter mines the resume to find candidate attributes that relate to the most important requirements of the role. Ideally, the job description will be written so that it is autism-friendly (see Chapter 7), but many job requirements can be viewed more inclusively, especially for entry-level jobs when a candidate has no paid work experience.

Candidate 2 graduated with a B.A. in Environmental Studies from a highly competitive school and has no paid work history. After college she looked for a job as a Project Manager or Field Technician for environmental science firms but has since expanded her search to a less specific role as a Research Assistant for a variety of organizations. Her resume is below:

Candidate 2 (Research Assistant)

Education

University of North Carolina   Chapel Hill, NC
B.A. in Environmental Studies, Minor in History – GPA 3.2   *May 2015*
Dean's List (Spring 2014): GPA 3.63

Work Experience

Center for Environmental Farming Systems   Raleigh, NC
Volunteer (Summer 2014)
Worked in the Small Farm Unit learning about sustainable
    food preparation

Pine Knoll Shores Aquarium   Pine Knoll Shores, NC
Intern (Summers 2012, 2013)
Presented lectures and provided information on a variety of
    exhibits

Capstone/Senior Seminar

Project on Hurricane Sandy
Presentation on impact of the storm and planning for the
    future
Developed coastal resilience, long-term strategic planning

Relevant Coursework

Weather and Climate
Natural Science and Environmental Problems
Social Science and Environmental Problems
Urban Environment
Physical Problems of Pollution
Biological Concepts and Methods 111, 112 (Lab Courses)
Environmental Geology
Human Evolution (Lab Course)

Skills

Public speaking
Proficient in PowerPoint, knowledgeable in MS Excel and
    Word

Here is an entry-level Research Assistant job description for a nonprofit in the health sector that could be a good fit for *Candidate 2* if viewed with an autism-friendly lens:

Job description: Research Assistant

Responsibilities:
- Performs research and/or development work under the guidance of an Associate or Assistant Investigator.

- Follows and adheres to experimental protocols in a proficient and meticulous manner.
- Responsible for the collection of data and may assist with analysis.
- Performs a variety of tasks, including completing correspondence, database maintenance, maintaining records, charts, etc.
- Participates in laboratory meetings and journal clubs as appropriate.

<u>Qualifications</u>:
- Bachelor's degree (required).
- Ability to communicate effectively.

Candidate 2 has the required bachelor's degree in a field related to the natural sciences. Her solid academic record and minor in History shows initiative. The summers of internship and Capstone project demonstrate the ability to research, write, and present information effectively, while completing several lab courses indicates that she is familiar with experimental protocols. When viewed holistically, a recruiter sourcing autistic candidates should see potential in her resume for this Research Assistant position.

For autistic college students, managing some of the challenges discussed in Chapters 4 and 5 as they pursue their post-secondary education makes the prospect of including work experience during the college years next to impossible. In reviewing resumes, if a candidate has no work experience, take that extra time – beyond those six seconds – to look for these other signs of dedication to developing strong skill sets and work readiness. What may initially appear as a candidate lacking experience may just be a candidate with autism whose knowledge and skill sets make them a good fit for the job.

The Job Hopper

While moving from one job or company to another is very common now, especially for Millennials, recruiters consider excessive "job hopping" a red flag. Some individuals on the autism spectrum do not struggle with the interview process and are successful at finding jobs. Their challenges arise once on the job when they might make social missteps at work, experience executive functioning challenges that are perceived as poor work performance, or struggle with anxiety that results in absences or other issues that interfere with their overall ability to complete their work. As a result, they will have resumes with multiple short stints of employment coupled with periods of unemployment and freelance assignments, making them appear to be "job hoppers". Typically, these individuals have not disclosed that they have a neurodivergent profile to prior employers or if they have, they have not received the support they need on the job to be successful. Their lack of success does not mean these candidates cannot become productive, long-term employees for your company. Supporting autistic new hires during the onboarding process will be covered later in Part IV.

Candidate 3 has a common job hopper's resume:

Candidate 3 *(Executive Assistant/Office Manager)*

Education

University of Southern California	Los Angeles, CA
B.S., Communications, minor English – GPA 3.0	May 2013

Skill Sets

Office management

- Budgeting and reconciliation for multiple office projects
- Implementation of updated and new software packages to improve efficiency, including full suite of Microsoft Office products
- Coordinate all travel and expense reimbursement for staff
- Oversee maintenance of all office equipment

General Business

- Assist senior management in drafting and editing of all internal and external memos, reports, and proposals
- Project management responsibility with budgets up to $10 million
- Track key metrics and performance, including interacting with internal and external auditors

Work Experience

Consultant, Los Angeles, CA	2015–present
J.Paul Getty Trust, *Executive Assistant*, Los Angeles, CA	June 2018–2019
Alston & Bird, *Office Manager*, Los Angeles, CA	2017
L.A. Health Care Plans, *Executive Assistant*, Los Angeles, CA	2015
Century Group, *Executive Assistant*, Los Angeles, CA	2014–2015

As you can see, after graduating from college, this individual embarked on a series of jobs as an Executive Assistant; however, he lists only the years he was employed, with no specific months. In most instances, this is an indication that the tenure of each job was shorter than 12 months and that the individual experienced gaps of unemployment between jobs. Additionally, *Candidate 3* began a consulting business in 2015 while continuing to hold different full-time positions, reinforcing the assumption that the positions listed were short-term and not successful. These are all red flags in recruiting and would likely result in *Candidate 3* being screened out in the standard resume review process discussed above.

The same approach should be taken with an autistic job hopper resume as with a resume with no relevant or paid work experience. First, recognize that *Candidate 3*'s experience demonstrates skills and capabilities that could be an asset to many Office Manager/Executive Assistant roles, as well as perseverance in continuing to seek appropriate employment. Second, when not working, *Candidate 3* seeks out freelance work to stay engaged and keep his skill sets up to date. As for the inability to retain a job, it will be important to understand why this individual could not maintain employment at any of his prior jobs. Many autistic individuals who present as job hoppers typically lose or leave their employment due to a lack of appropriate support, either because they have not disclosed their autism or their employer cannot/will not provide the support they need. In Chapter 11 we discuss interview questions and provide some suggestions of how to ask job hoppers about their work history. For more guidance about how to support autistic employees, see our companion book, *An Employer's Guide to Managing Professionals on the Autism Spectrum*.

Conclusion

Appropriate roles exist for autistic employees across all business levels and functions; however, the stereotype that all individuals on the spectrum would be good computer programmers is a limiting factor in employment opportunities for autistic jobseekers. Coupled with a lack of relevant work experience on the part of many candidates on the spectrum and the dependence on social communication skills of most interview processes, it is no wonder autistic individuals struggle to find work.

The interview process starts with recruiters reviewing candidate resumes for specific roles. To be inclusive of autistic candidates, employers need to think broadly about the roles they can fill. Reviewing resumes "horizontally" will help identify autistic candidates that demonstrate dedication and determination in acquiring skills in a variety of ways, not just through traditional job experience.

Notes

1 Lime. "Leading Perspectives on Disability: A Q&A with Dr. Stephen Shore." March 22, 2018. https://www.limeconnect.com/opportunities_news/detail/leadin g-perspectives-on-disability-a-qa-with-dr-stephen-shore.
2 Turczynski, Bart. "2020 HR Statistics: Job Search, Hiring, Recruiting & Interviews." *Zsety*, November 15, 2016. https://zety.com/blog/hr-statistics.
3 Qu, Linda. "99% of Fortune 500 Companies Use Applicant Tracking Systems (ATS)." *Jobscan Blog* (blog), November 7, 2019. https://www.jobscan.co/blog /99-percent-fortune-500-ats/.

Chapter 7

Does Your Company Embrace Neurodiversity?

In 2016, the Return on Disability Group published a report on *The Global Economics of Disability*. It is not surprising that they found that companies that employ more people with disabilities perform better financially. They also found these same organizations followed two guiding principles to attract and retain people with disabilities. First, "one size does not fit all" when thinking about engaging the disability community.[1] Over 70% of people with disabilities have an invisible disability, such as learning or cognitive disabilities.[2] As an employer, it is important to recognize the diversity within disability, and develop an understanding of the needs of different types of disabled individuals.

Second, efforts to hire people with disabilities "require a laser beam focus on business drivers first, with 'social' factors in the background".[3] A person with disabilities does not want to be thought of as a "charity" hire: they want to be contributing members of their organization. Therefore, the long-term success of a hire in an organization depends on that employee's ability to fill a business need for their employer.

Keeping these two principles in mind, an organization's process of integrating autistic jobseekers into its workforce starts with an open attitude toward neurodiversity that permeates the company's culture and creates an environment where employees feel safe disclosing, if they so choose. This chapter outlines a "disability-friendly" hiring process that starts with reaching out to the autistic community in a transparent fashion to attract talent. Then it covers how to write job descriptions that accurately reflect the essential components of a role without unintentionally discouraging autistic applicants, as well as how to tailor the application process.

Appeal to the Broader Autism Community

The autism community does not consist of just those individuals with an autism spectrum diagnosis, but also family and friends who care for and support them. As mentioned in Chapter 2, the current incidence rate of one in 54 children[4] and 5.4 million adults[5] being diagnosed on the autism spectrum means approximately 6.78 million autistic individuals are living in the US, and each of them may have 1.85 family members/friends.[6] Using this conservative estimate, the "autism market" calculates to 19.3 million people or 5.8% of the US population. As an employer, you want to be known to this community as being autism friendly in all your business practices. Whether you are trying to attract employees or customers, your reputation with these two constituencies will have a major impact on your success. If you want to have autistic employees, you need to appeal to the broader autism community by thinking holistically: autistic individuals and their families and friends can interact with your organization in many ways – as customers, suppliers, and employees.

Customer Outreach

Let's start with *customer outreach* by assessing how your organization communicates with the autistic community through the media, your website, and your products. First, apply concepts of *universal design*[7] to make sure your avenues of communication to the marketplace are accessible, ensuring that the language you use in all types of marketing materials (print, TV, and social media) can be easily read and understood by all. Individuals with autism and other neurodivergent conditions may struggle with verbal processing and reading. Therefore, communications should not include complex sentences, metaphors, jargon, and run-on paragraphs.[8] Guidelines provided on the US government's Plain Language Initiative website address crafting clear communications for the public.[9] The presentation of information should also be easily readable, with a focus on high contrast colors and multiple formats of information delivery. The US government's Americans with Disabilities Act (ADA) website provides a toolkit on website accessibility.[10]

Second, if your company sells to the general public, develop or adapt products that will service the disability marketplace. Global brands have now joined specialized companies in this initiative, such as Marks & Spencer and Tommy Hilfiger – two clothing manufacturers that have designed adaptive clothing lines for people with both physical and mental disabilities. Procter & Gamble's Herbal Essence hair care products are available in bottles for those with vision impairments.[11] Microsoft launched a program – AI for Accessibility – to support the development of technologies focused on employment, daily life, and communication for people with disabilities.[12] Nike's FlyEase laceless shoes, inspired by a customer with cerebral palsy, have found a wide market among people with and without disabilities.[13]

In the autism market, AMC Theatres offers movie screenings designed to be sensory friendly for autistic people twice a month.[14] Several specialized manufacturers produce lines of tagless clothing and some supermarkets offer sensory-friendly shopping hours. Major brands have found that some of their standard merchandise appeals to those with sensory sensitivities: fragrance-free toiletries and cleaning products, soft clothing with flat seams, and noise-canceling headsets. Business product Trello, a flexible task management application inspired by sticky notes, has been implemented at Spectrum Designs (staffed by over 75% autistic employees) as part of their inclusive, visual workplace. In a story featured on Trello's company blog, founder Michael Pryor states, "We always say that Trello can be whatever you make it, and I'm so happy to see it being used in such an important way".[15]

Supplier Diversity Programs

The arguments for focusing on *supplier diversity* to attract and retain a diverse workforce are very much the same as those already discussed in Chapter 2 around brand recognition and employee engagement. Where a company sources its necessary supplies, whatever they may be, can be a factor in purchasing decisions by consumers and employment choices by individuals. The US Census projects that by 2045, over 50% of the US population will be non-white majority,[16] driven by the growth and diversity of the youth population, who look for organizations that reflect their values when making decisions about where to shop and work.[17]

As consumers increasingly use social media to share their values and purchasing habits, employers will need to meet their supply needs as well as appeal to the next generation of potential employees (disabled or not) by demonstrating supplier diversity to the marketplace. Organizations implementing *supplier diversity programs* and the disability-owned business enterprises (DOBEs) that supply them can both benefit from showcasing partnerships and company values on their respective Diversity and Inclusion webpages. For example, DOBE Spectrum Designs supplies custom apparel and promotional products to clients such as Google, Uber, and Northwell Health. According to Dupont's Supplier Diversity page, "ensuring our supply base reflects our customers, employees, and the communities where we live and work is a key business strategy".[18] A similar page on Adobe's site says that they are "aligning our spending with our values ... [and] using our purchasing power to promote the things we care about as a company".[19]

Become an Employer of Choice

As with customers, clear messaging is critical when trying to attract potential job candidates who are neurodivergent: you want to be known as an *employer of choice*. In Chapter 1, we touched on some techniques for creating an environment where autistic employees feel safe disclosing if they choose to do so; these same strategies apply for creating an environment to attract autistic jobseekers. Whether or not an autistic individual wants to disclose their disability to their employer, they will be more inclined to apply to an organization that demonstrates an understanding and acceptance of the needs of autistic individuals.

Company Website and Resource Groups

If you have an autism hiring effort, consider creating a separate landing page for it on the Careers page of your website, as well as the Diversity and Inclusion page, and make it easy to find. Include as much information as possible for jobseekers. For example, Microsoft had two programs for autistic individuals – one at their retail stores which closed in 2020 and another active program in their corporate offices. They have multiple access points on their website to the link for the corporate hiring program. The site features:

- Stories about current employees on the spectrum
- A description of the interview process
- A listing of upcoming hiring events and job openings
- A Q&A section with a sign-up option for a monthly newsletter

The website uses a combination of text and video to appeal to a broad range of processing styles.[20] All of these features reflect sensitivity to the issues raised in Chapters 4 and 5 around communication styles and the need for *previewing* the job search and application process.

Many organizations support business resource groups (BRGs) or employee resource groups (ERGs) to foster greater inclusion for employees who share a common identity and empower them to drive initiatives within their organization. While most large employers have a BRG or ERG for people with disabilities and their caregivers and allies, more and more of these resources are beginning to include a specific focus on autism. For example, Capital One has Advocacy Circles as part of their CapAbilities BRG, with one of those Advocacy Circles being Autism Spectrum Connections.[21] These groups can be instrumental in creating broader autism awareness and acceptance in your organization by hosting events and training sessions, as well as advocating for hiring programs. BRG/ERG members can also become advocates in the community for your organization, developing that greater reach your organization needs as it becomes known as an autism-friendly employer.

Publicity is Good for Recruiting

Whatever your organization may be doing to create a neurodivergent-friendly workplace, potential employees will not know if you don't tell them. We encounter many employers who say they do not want to publicize their autism hiring initiatives, as they believe publicizing is asking for public praise for an initiative they should be engaged in regardless. Our response: *publicity is not bragging, and it's good for business and recruiting.* A quick scan of YouTube will show that some of the employers with the largest neurodiversity-hiring initiatives – SAP, Microsoft, JPMorgan Chase, Dell, and Ford – have videos posted about their efforts. A search in Google on the names of the employees who lead the Autism@Work programs at SAP, JPMorgan Chase, and EY generates pages of news articles and links to speaking engagements, as they travel the country talking about the benefits of neurodiversity hiring. This publicity is an integral part of making their organizations known as autism-friendly and increasing their pipeline of autistic candidates.

Publicity not only helps to create a reputation externally as an autism-friendly workplace; it will facilitate goodwill internally. Undisclosed autistic employees may feel more inclined to come forward when they see their employer actively hiring and supporting autistic peers. Employees with a personal connection to autism experience a sense of pride in their employer. SAP, an early adopter of Autism@Work hiring, believes their efforts around inclusiveness lead to increased employee engagement and more: their internal model tells them that for every point increase in employee engagement they experience a \$40–50 million increase in revenue.[22]

Avoid Job Description Jargon

The first interaction many job candidates have with an employer is a job posting, yet it is often the first barrier they encounter. A 2019 study by LinkedIn showed that women searching for jobs are more likely than men to screen themselves out of an opportunity, based on the job description, and as a result, apply to 20% fewer jobs than men. The LinkedIn report goes on to recommend:

> To encourage women to apply, be thoughtful about what you put in your job postings. Roles with endless lists of requirements, nice-to-haves, and strict seniority demands can deter women from applying as they often want to make sure they check every box you list … (F)ocus on what are the performance objectives of the role and what the person will be expected to accomplish. This approach will give candidates a more realistic idea of the job and attract people with a non-traditional skill set and experiences.[23]

This advice applies to attracting autistic candidates as well.

Autistic individuals can be very literal in their reading of job descriptions: see Chapter 5 for a more in-depth discussion of *literal thinking*. This, in combination with their tendency to undervalue their skill sets, deters them from applying to many jobs for which they are qualified, as described by these three autistic professionals:

> If I see a job description that says, "excellent communication skills", I absolutely will not apply for it. If they say, "excellent written communication skills", I will apply for it.
>
> When a job description lists multiple items, I'm not going to try to decipher which items are more valid for that specific position. I'm going to assume they're all there for a reason, and all have equal priority.
>
> There were a lot of ads that would say, "strong interpersonal and communication skills required". It's like saying that they didn't want me to apply.

One of the first steps in a successful recruiting process for autistic candidates is to have job descriptions that:

- Are clearly written
- Do not include acronyms or company-specific jargon
- Provide enough context for candidates
- Include only the essential requirements for the job

When working with employers, we spend a great deal of time refining job descriptions before beginning outreach for candidates. Every job description should include the following component parts:

Company/Division Description
This can be at the beginning or end of the posting.

Position Title
Include a description of where the role fits into the organization. For example, "Staff Accountant supporting the financial reporting team in the finance division".

Responsibilities or Core Responsibilities

- List only those things the candidate will do on a regular basis in the role.
- Avoid acronyms and company-specific jargon.

Skills/Requirements
List only those items necessary for a candidate to be considered for the position:
  - Pay attention to *experience levels* required and how that experience might be demonstrated in non-traditional ways.
  - Think about the required *soft skills* and their relevance to the level of the job: "leadership skills" may not be necessary for entry-level or individual contributor roles. Many job descriptions list "team

player" as a standard requirement. If teamwork is a key feature of a role, be more specific as to how the candidate will be required to interact with colleagues. For example, "ability to work collaboratively with team members within the group and from other departments on projects" or "will be required on a periodic basis to work with multiple team members".

- Clarify very specific *academic or technical skill requirements*. Keep in mind that too much specificity will screen out potentially qualified candidates.

Diversity and Inclusion Statement/Policy

Many, but not all, employers include a statement on their job descriptions that addresses their policies on non-discrimination and equal employment opportunity. If your company has policies in these areas, include them on your job descriptions. Below is a sample of one of the most comprehensive descriptions of a non-discrimination policy we have seen included by an employer:

Company XYZ is an Equal Opportunity Employer. We seek candidates without regard to age, race, color, ancestry, national origin, citizenship status, military or veteran status, religion, creed, disability, sex, sexual orientation, marital status, medical condition as defined by applicable law, genetic information, gender, gender identity, gender expression, pregnancy, childbirth and related medical conditions, or any other characteristic protected by applicable federal, state, or local laws and ordinances.

Special Features

If you are willing to offer benefits or features of the job that are not typical, such as flextime or the ability to work remotely, state that on the job description. These are options that might appeal to an autistic candidate who struggles with anxiety (see Chapter 4 for more information on anxiety).

Every organization has its own style, and job descriptions should reflect that style. As long as the above information is incorporated into a job description, autistic candidates should have the information they need to make an informed decision as to whether or not they are qualified to apply. In the Appendix section of this book, you will find samples of job descriptions that we have used with client companies that are well-written for an autistic job-seeker (Examples 7.1 and 7.2), as well as a sample job description with the changes we recommended to make it autism friendly (Example 7.3 Before and 7.4 After). A common theme in all three examples – short and to the point.

In the "before" job description (Example 7.3), recommended changes are highlighted in italics; Example 7.4 shows the revised job description. In addition to adding some of the sections discussed above, the key changes to note are those under Core Responsibilities and Skills/Requirements:

- Under Core Responsibilities (or any responsibilities in a job description), if the employee will be working with or subordinate to other team members on certain activities, be sure to say that. Autistic individuals are likely to self-select out if they believe they will be solely responsible for tasks they have not done before.
- Under Skills/Requirements, be as specific as possible about the desired skill sets needed for the job. If a job requires an individual to communicate with others, rather than asking for an "effective communicator", state "ability to communicate with others effectively in writing or verbally". This appeals to a candidate who may struggle with social interactions yet writes very clearly.

Overall, avoid requirements that are vague, subjective, and/or difficult for the applicant to quantify or evaluate, such as "ability to influence", "add significant value", or "substantial experience".

Simplify the Application Maze

The process of looking and applying for a job is daunting, even for the most confident and organized individuals. For autistic jobseekers, the social and organizational demands of looking for a job can be overwhelming. After deciphering the job posting, the next barrier to entry to the employment world for autistic individuals may be the application process itself. As a result, many individuals on the spectrum will give up before finding appropriate employment. Having a simple and clear process for applying to your organization for open positions will not only increase your pipeline of all neurodivergent candidates but likely increase your pool of all potential candidates.

Today, almost 90% of candidates begin the job application process by applying online,[24] whether it be directly with the hiring organization, a social media site, or through a third-party staffing company. In a 2015 study of 427 jobseekers with disabilities conducted by the Partnership on Employment & Accessible Technology (PEAT), 46% rated their last experience applying online for a job as "difficult to impossible". The issues with online application systems raised by these job applicants included "complex navigation" and "timeout restrictions".[25] In fact, many job candidates, disabled or not, complain that the online job application process can be extremely frustrating. Common complaints include:

- Most online systems require the candidate to submit a resume, yet also ask the candidate to re-enter much of the same information into preset forms.
- The systems may or may not allow candidates to submit cover letters, and oftentimes do not indicate if a cover letter is desirable or not.

- Once a candidate has completed the online application, they do not receive any confirmation that the application has been received.[26]

The application process becomes significantly more difficult for jobseekers who rely on smartphones and tablets. According to a recent study by job recruiting site Glassdoor, 58% of their users are looking for jobs on their phones, yet these candidates, on average, successfully complete 53% fewer applications and take 80% longer to complete each application! As mobile job search usage increases, so will the need for a mobile-friendly online application process.[27]

For autistic candidates, the frustration experienced with the application process may be magnified by challenges with executive functioning, processing differences, and anxiety, as discussed in Chapters 4 and 5. To avoid having autistic jobseekers self-select out at this stage of the process, employing a universal design strategy can make the application process more accessible for neurodivergent candidates and neurotypical jobseekers alike. Key elements of universal design to consider for autistic individuals in the job application process include:

Previewing the Application Process:

- Provide a description of what the candidate will have to complete throughout the entire application process, so they can gather any required materials beforehand, including any technical tests they may be required to take and any time limits on completing any portion(s) of the application. If time limits are being imposed on any portion of the application process, including any technical tests, explain why the time limit is necessary and provide clear information on how to request an accommodation to have time limits changed and/or removed.
- If you require drug testing at any time during your process, say so upfront, as some candidates take medications that may need to be disclosed to pass drug tests.

Displaying Information on Requesting Accommodations:

- This information should be placed upfront in the materials, with clear instructions on how to request an accommodation and when the candidate should expect to hear back about their request.
- Candidates should be instructed to read the preview of the application process before requesting any accommodations, so they have a full understanding of the process and can request all desired accommodations upfront.

Instructions in Multiple Formats:

– Neurodivergent candidates will vary in the way they process information.
– Provide instructions in text, infographic, and video formats, allowing candidates to choose the format that best suits their processing style.

For more guidance on how to create an inclusive recruiting process for people with disabilities, visit the website of the Office of Disability Employment Policy's (ODEP's) Job Accommodation Network.[28]

Conclusion

Employers that are truly successful in creating an inclusive workplace for autistic employees think holistically about being a neurodiverse-friendly organization. *Employers of choice* focus not only on their hiring and management practices for autistic individuals but on how they engage with all their stakeholders in the neurodivergent community. Additionally, even before inviting candidates to interview with their organization, these companies make sure their outreach – through appealing to the broader autism community, job descriptions, and application processes – is designed to attract and support autistic jobseekers. Not only do these companies have a higher percentage of employees with disabilities, they perform better financially.

Notes

1 Return on Disability Group. *2016 Annual Report – The Global Economics of Disability*. May 2016. https://www.rod-group.com/content/rod-research/edit-res earch-2016-annual-report-global-economics-disability, 11.
2 Steinmetz, Erika. "U.S. Census Bureau Current Population Report: Americans with Disabilities: 2002." *US Census Bureau*. May 2006. https://www.census.gov /prod/2006pubs/p70-107.pdf.
3 Return on Disability Group, *2016 Annual Report – The Global Economics of Disability*, 21.
4 CDC. "Data and Statistics on Autism Spectrum Disorder." *Centers for Disease Control and Prevention*, March 25, 2020. https://www.cdc.gov/ncbddd/autism/d ata.html.
5 CDC. "Key Findings: CDC Releases First Estimates of the Number of Adults Living with Autism Spectrum Disorder in the United States." *Centers for Disease Control and Prevention*, April 27, 2020. https://www.cdc.gov/ncbddd/autism/f eatures/adults-living-with-autism-spectrum-disorder.html.
6 Return on Disability Group, *2016 Annual Report – The Global Economics of Disability*, 11.
7 Universal Design (UD) is a strategy for making an environment welcoming and usable to the most diverse range of people possible. Its key principles are simplicity, flexibility, and efficiency.
8 Hawkins, Jon. "How to Write Disability-Friendly Content." *Medium*, May 18, 2020. https://medium.com/better-marketing/how-to-write-disability-friendly-c ontent-277845b8c2ee.

9 Plain Language. "Federal Plain Language Guidelines." March 10, 2021. https://www.plainlanguage.gov/guidelines/.

10 ADA. "ADA Tool Kit: Website Accessibility Under Title II of the ADA." August 30, 2020. https://www.ada.gov/pcatoolkit/chap5toolkit.htm.

11 Hammett, Ellen. "What Brands Are Doing to Be More Inclusive for People with Disabilities." *Marketing Week* (blog), February 6, 2019. https://www.marketingweek.com/how-brands-are-being-more-inclusive-for-people-with-disabilities/.

12 Microsoft. "AI for Accessibility – Microsoft AI." August 30, 2020. https://www.microsoft.com/en-us/ai/ai-for-accessibility.

13 Casey, Caroline. "Do Your D&I Efforts Include People with Disabilities?" *Harvard Business Review*, March 19, 2020. https://hbr.org/2020/03/do-your-di-efforts-include-people-with-disabilities.

14 AMC. "Sensory Friendly Films." August 30, 2020. https://www.amctheatres.com/programs/sensory-friendly-films.

15 Ryder, Leah. "How a T-Shirt Company Built an Inclusive, Visual Workplace with Trello." August 30, 2020. https://blog.trello.com/how-spectrum-designs-built-inclusive-visual-workplace-with-trello.

16 PBS NewsHour. "3 Ways That the U.S. Population Will Change over the Next Decade." January 2, 2020. https://www.pbs.org/newshour/nation/3-ways-that-the-u-s-population-will-change-over-the-next-decade.

17 Michigan State University. "Why Diversity Is Important in Supply Chain Management." *MSU Online*, September 28, 2018. https://www.michiganstateuniversityonline.com/resources/supply-chain/the-importance-of-diverse-suppliers/.

18 Dupont. "Supplier Diversity." February 1, 2021. https://www.dupont.com/supplier-center/supplier-diversity.html.

19 Adobe. "Adobe Supplier Diversity." March 30, 2020. https://www.adobe.com/diversity/strategy/industry/suppliers.html.

20 Microsoft. "Autism Hiring Corporate." August 31, 2020. https://www.microsoft.com/en-us/diversity/inside-microsoft/cross-disability/autismhiringcorporate.

21 Capital One. "Diversity, Inclusion & Belonging." August 31, 2020. https://www.capitalone.com/diversity/business-resource-groups/.

22 Segal, R. P. "SAP Develops Workforce of the Future." October 6, 2020. https://www.triplepundit.com/story/2015/sap-develops-workforce-future/57881.

23 LinkedIn. "New Report: Women Apply to Fewer Jobs Than Men, But Are More Likely to Get Hired." August 31, 2020. https://business.linkedin.com/talent-solutions/blog/diversity/2019/how-women-find-jobs-gender-report.

24 Partnership on Employment & Accessible Technology. "PEAT: Accessible Technology & The Employment Lifecycle." 2017. YouTube video, 2:46. https://www.youtube.com/watch?v=45mkpIMkl-M.

25 Partnership on Employment & Accessible Technology. "Infographic: The Accessibility of Online Job Applications." *Peatworks* (blog). August 31, 2020. https://peatworks.org/digital-accessibility-toolkits/talentworks/make-your-erecruiting-tools-accessible/new-data-on-the-accessibility-of-online-job-applications/.

26 Kelly, Jack. "11 Complaints from Frustrated and Angry Job Seekers about the Interview Process." *Forbes*. August 31, 2020. https://www.forbes.com/sites/jackkelly/2019/08/12/11-complaints-from-frustrated-and-angry-job-seekers-about-the-interview-process/.

27 Glassdoor Economic Research. "The Rise of Mobile Devices in Job Search: Challenges and Opportunities for Employers." June 3, 2019. https://www.glassdoor.com/research/mobile-job-search/.

28 ODEP. "Job Accommodation Network." *Office of Disability Employment Policy*, August 31, 2020. https://askjan.org/.

Chapter 8

Sourcing Autistic Jobseekers

In 2019, a group of employers with established neurodiversity hiring programs published the *Autism@Work Playbook* in which they noted the most critical factor to the success of an Autism@Work program is the ability to source talent. The playbook goes on to advise employers "to own their sourcing function and leverage a wide range of channels" if they want to find the desired talent.[1] As discussed in Chapter 3, however, even the authors of the *Autism@Work Playbook* – the companies most experienced at recruiting neurodivergent talent – have struggled to meet their originally stated hiring goals for autistic individuals. As with all aspects of attracting and retaining employees with an atypical way of thinking, one must use non-traditional outreach methods to source autistic jobseekers.

Campus recruiting, the internet, social media, sourcing partners, and community outreach are all familiar recruiting avenues for employers as shown in Figure 8.1. These outlets can continue to be used to reach autistic candidates, but employers need to think more creatively about how they do so. This chapter will address how to "speak to" autistic jobseekers through the available recruiting outlets and source candidates through these outlets in non-traditional ways.

Campus Recruiting

For entry-level and early career talent, many large employers look to colleges and universities as their main pipeline of talent. The career services offices of colleges and universities make it very easy for employers to access their students and find a wide range of available talent. However, the process of engaging with career services can oftentimes be overwhelming for students on the autism spectrum, making it difficult for employers to recruit a candidate pool that includes autistic talent through traditional college recruiting strategies.

Autistic college students are often singularly focused on their academics when in college. While many may excel academically, they typically need to create a highly structured environment and routine for themselves, eliminating or minimizing distractions and activities not related to coursework. For

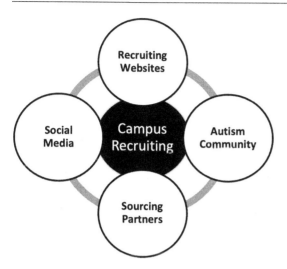

Figure 8.1 Sources for Autistic Jobseekers.

those who need accommodations, they will register with their school's disability services office, and use that as their main source of support during their time on campus. As a result, some autistic students will not think about employment while pursuing their degree and never visit career services during their college days.

For autistic students who do go to career services, many have little success. The reason for this is twofold. First, most career service counselors are not trained in supporting the needs of autistic students and therefore may not provide them with effective job search guidance. Also, at most colleges and universities, since career services and disability services have little to no interaction, career services may not have the understanding of an autistic student's needs that could be provided by disability services, particularly those students who may come to career services but not disclose. Second, the measure of success for career services offices is their placement rate. Given they may be short on resources, this incentivizes them to focus on those students who seek their support and actively follow their advice. As mentioned above, many autistic college students are mainly focused on their schoolwork and struggle to conduct a full-fledged job search at the same time.

As a result, it is important to engage with disability services as well as career services at your target schools. Even this can be a scattershot approach, as disability services doesn't require that students disclose their actual disability; many neurodivergent students will register with disability services to receive accommodations, such as extra time and a quiet room for taking exams, but not disclose their diagnosis. Fortunately, there are other avenues on campus that may allow you to attract autistic students on campus more effectively.

Autism Support Programs

It is estimated that approximately 2% of college/university students today are autistic.[2] To respond to the growing number of students with an autism spectrum disorder (ASD) on college campuses, a number of schools have established specialized support programs for these students:

- *College Autism Spectrum*, a consulting firm that works with students and parents, lists 70 college and university support programs throughout the US on their website,[3] and this number is growing.
- *Top College Consultants*, another consulting organization for students with autism and learning differences who are looking for the right college environment, lists over 145 colleges and universities on their website that provide some type of support for autistic students.[4]
- *College Autism Network (CAN)*, a nonprofit whose goal is to maximize the success of autistic students and the colleges that support them, has a published list of 82 colleges and universities throughout the US with autism support programs.[5]

The size and quality of these college-based programs vary, but most have dedicated staff trained in supporting autistic individuals academically and socially. Additionally, some of these programs have staff members dedicated to job placement services for their autistic students.

When transitioning into or out of college, some autistic individuals want a more supportive living environment before taking the step of living independently in a dormitory or apartment. For these individuals, comprehensive residential, school, and work programs – often referred to as *wrap-around transition programs* – exist. At these programs, students receive independent living and work readiness skills training, while attending local colleges and universities. Some of these programs also provide academic/technical training for their students. Going directly to autism support programs on college and university campuses, as well as to transition programs, will provide access to a disclosed talent pool of autistic candidates, with the added benefit of support from program staff who can guide you in providing the candidates with a successful interview experience.

Campus Events

Other typical avenues for connecting with students on campus include job fairs and hosting special events for targeted groups, such as a pharmaceutical company that hosts an event for the Chemistry Club. When seeking potential employees through a socially-based event, keep in mind that many autistic individuals find these types of social interactions difficult and anxiety provoking, and therefore will not attend. There are social events, however, that can draw an autistic audience.

Not all autistic individuals will present the same. No two individuals on the spectrum are affected by autism the same way, and the behaviors they demonstrate related to autism will be unique to them.

In our experience, we find some autistic college students who participate in extracurricular activities belong to video game, board game, or anime clubs. Host a video game night; allowing potential candidates to play games with your recruiters while engaging in conversation in a less formal manner (see sample invitation in Figure 8.2). Such an evening could include employees from your company with an interest in video games, where students belonging to the Video Game Club are asked to bring their resumes to the event.

COMPANY XYZ SPONSORS
UNIVERSITY OF MINNESOTA'S

 **Pwn Gaming Club**

COME PLAY

Animal Crossing: New Horizons
Final Fantasy VII Remake
or bring your favorite game

Thursday, September 17, 2020, 7-9 p.m.
Kirby Student Center, Room 204

Come have fun and network!

If you're looking for a job, bring your resume too

Refreshments will be served.

Figure 8.2 Sample Video Game Night Invitation.

In between rounds of games, your employees can engage in more casual conversation with their gaming partners about their career goals.

Similarly, show an anime movie and facilitate a group discussion about the movie afterward. This will serve as an icebreaker and some individuals will want to stay on to continue discussions, which you could then steer toward career goals. Invite the chess club for a tournament. Again, this will allow students and recruiters to have an alternative point of focus as they get to know each other and establish a rapport. These suggestions do play on some stereotypes of the interests of autistic individuals and do not guarantee that the individuals who attend are on the spectrum, but all emphasize the same concept: if you want to attract autistic candidates to your campus events, you need to offer an interesting activity in a low-stress environment.

Effective Use of the Internet

In Chapter 7 we discussed how to make your website neurodivergent friendly, but the internet includes many more ways to reach autistic candidates. While it is well known that up to 80% of individuals find their jobs through networking,[6] almost all jobseekers spend a lot of time looking for and applying to postings online.

In a 2020 survey conducted by Jobvite, they found that almost all recruiters use some form of social media to find candidates. The four most popular social media sites for recruiters are LinkedIn (72%), Facebook (60%), Twitter (38%), and Instagram (37%).[7] These sites, along with job board sites, can all be useful in attracting neurodivergent talent; however, keep in mind that they are typically designed for neurotypical individuals. Therefore, it is important to ask, "Is my approach inclusive?" when using social media and recruiting sites (i.e., Glassdoor, Monster, CareerBuilder, Dice, and Indeed).

Social Media

Recruiters oftentimes use the same approach when screening a candidate's social media profile that they do when screening a candidate's resume. For example, the following information tends to be the focus of recruiters when reviewing someone's information on LinkedIn:

- How long a job is held on average
- Length of time with the current employer
- Mutual connections and the candidate's business (industry) connections
- Searchability (particularly on LinkedIn because keyword optimization improves searchability)
- A personality that is well articulated online[8]

As with the standard resume review process discussed in Chapter 6, this approach will likely exclude, rather than include, autistic individuals in your candidate pool. First, it is important to screen using metrics that will be relevant for neurodivergent talent. A more appropriate list for autistic individuals might include:

- Skills
- Academic achievements
- Examples of work
- Companies/individuals they follow
- Extracurricular activities they pursue, keeping in mind some individuals may have had limited involvement with extracurricular activities due to their hyperfocus on their academics

Second, when searching for candidates, particularly on career sites such as LinkedIn, use the terms "autism", "autistic", "neurodiverse", and "neurodivergent". Some autistic individuals participate in programs and organizations that support autistic and/or neurodivergent individuals and will list them on their profiles; this can be an indication that a candidate is on the autism spectrum. For example, some colleges and universities offer their autistic students peer counselors who are also on the spectrum. An individual may list being such a peer counselor on their LinkedIn profile and/or resume, not only to demonstrate their experience in this area but to disclose that they are autistic. It is a neurotypical misconception that most autistic candidates view autism as a disadvantage: many candidates attribute their skills and talents to autism and, rightly, value it as a result.

Today, most companies have Facebook, Twitter, and Instagram accounts. These can be active recruiting sources for your organization. Just as you should use your website and employee resource groups/business resource groups to become an employer of choice (as discussed in Chapter 7), your social media accounts are powerful tools to promote your diversity and inclusion programs and highlight autism hiring initiatives. Feature stories of neurodivergent employees, and always have a link to your careers site in your postings.

Recruiting Websites

When selecting vendors that host online job boards, it is important to view them through the same lens you use on your own recruiting process, as discussed previously in Chapter 7. Some key considerations include:

- Is the site designed with the principles of universal design?
- Are the search parameters clearly defined and explained for jobseekers so they can easily find postings?

- Is the application process for candidates straightforward?
- Are instructions written in a clear and concise manner? Are visual aids used as well?
- Do applicants have to upload a resume and then enter the same information multiple times?
- Does the site provide candidates the opportunity to disclose a disability if they so choose?
- What are the site's own policies and practices around hiring people with disabilities (in this case, neurodivergent individuals)?

If in asking the questions above you find your favorite recruiting sites do not appear to be particularly autism friendly, talk to your customer service representative about your goal of attracting neurodivergent candidates through their site and any concerns you have identified that may limit your ability to do so. This type of feedback can be powerful in encouraging these sites to make the necessary changes to their platforms to attract autistic jobseekers.

A few recruiting websites have been created specifically for autistic jobseekers. These sites allow individuals to post their resumes and employers to post open roles, with the goal of connecting the two. While these sites do offer employers a way to identify autistic talent, they may have their limitations. First, these websites provide a matching system primarily based on resumes and job roles. As such they do not offer employers the benefit of working with someone who knows and has specifically referred an individual. Second, these sites provide little to no guidance to employers on how to appropriately evaluate and provide a successful interview process to candidates. Third, it is unclear what controls these sites have to prevent non-autistic candidates from posting their resumes or employers who are looking to hire autistic workers at below-market wages from posting jobs.

Sourcing Partners

Several types of organizations exist to support employers in sourcing persons with disabilities (PWD). Most of these organizations represent all PWD and serve the individual as their primary client, while others specialize in supporting companies that want to implement their own targeted autism hiring program. As a result, for employers looking specifically to hire autistic talent, it is important to understand the different roles each of these partners plays, what they can offer, and how to best utilize their services. To be successful in finding autistic candidates, it is best to work with multiple partners over time. Just as very few organizations would limit their outsourced recruiting efforts to one partner, for hiring talent on the spectrum it is most effective to consider using multiple sourcing partners.

Vocational Agencies

US citizens with a disability are entitled to vocational support services from the government. This is accomplished through a state-based vocational rehabilitation (VR) system. Individuals register with their local state agency office, then receive services in one of two ways. They may receive employment services directly from an employee of the state or be referred to a private, state-funded agency specializing in employment services for autistic individuals. Regardless, to source candidates through this system, employers need to identify the state VR offices and private agencies in the locations they wish to recruit. As you work with VR, keep in mind that the candidates they suggest will be limited to their *existing* clients. These agencies will not go out into the market to source candidates if they do not have clients that can fill your hiring needs.

Employers report mixed experience with VR. In a 2018 study completed by the General Accounting Office, it was found that "(e)mployers in one of four discussion groups said that VR does not always provide enough qualified job candidates to meet their needs, and employers in another discussion group said that job candidates referred by VR are not always good matches for their hiring needs".[9] Additionally, if you are working with vocational agencies, keep in mind that not everyone with autism, particularly college graduates, registers with their state VR agency, as many autistic college graduates find they are placed in low-skill, low-pay jobs when they do register with their state VR system.

Despite the need to navigate the state-based VR system and the limitation of potential candidates, employers should not ignore vocational agencies as a source of autistic talent. Because the system is so fractured, the quality of service will not only vary greatly by state, but greatly within a state. Some VR agencies, particularly the private, state-funded ones, have developed a specialty in serving the autism population.

Utilizing other avenues of sourcing partners – autism employment experts, members of the Autism@Work Roundtable, and the autism community – will be helpful in identifying which VR organizations may be the most productive to work with, as they all have experience with VR agencies.

Autism Employment Experts

In the past few years, many organizations and individuals have established themselves as experts in the field of autism employment. These experts provide a range of services including consulting on how to best establish an autism hiring initiative; training and educating companies on how to recruit, interview, and manage neurodivergent talent; sourcing candidates; and supporting managers and neurodivergent employees post-hire. When sourcing autistic talent, tap into these experts. However, ask if the expert you are working with is representing a group of candidates he/she is seeking to place in jobs, as is the case with VR agencies, or tapping into a broader autistic talent pool to find the right candidates for you. Also, ask how transparent the expert's recruiting process will be to you so that over time you will learn how to source candidates on your own. See Chapter 3 for a list of questions to ask the organizations/professionals you are considering as partners.

US Government and National Associations

The US government sponsors a program called the Workforce Recruitment Program (WRP). Employers can register to access a database of approximately 2,000 current college students and graduates with disabilities. Annually, trained WRP recruiters from federal agencies conduct personal interviews with interested candidates from college and university campuses across the country. Candidates who interview successfully are included in the database, which is made available to employers each December. The database is renewed with a fresh set of candidates every year.[10]

If looking specifically to source candidates for an autism hiring initiative, this may be a difficult way to clearly identify autistic candidates as individuals' disabilities are not identified. Obviously, any candidate you choose will have a disability, but it is not guaranteed that you will be able to determine from the information on their resume that they are on the spectrum. However, it is an easily accessible, free source of candidates with disabilities.

Two additional summer internship programs targeted at college students with disabilities are sponsored by the American Association for the Advancement of Science (AAAS) and the American Association of People with Disabilities (AAPD). AAAS' program – called Entry Point! – asks employers to provide ten-week summer internships for college students with apparent and non-apparent disabilities wishing to pursue a STEM career.[11] AAPD also wants employers to provide a summer internship for college students and recent graduates with disabilities in a variety of functions.[12] As with the WRP, these programs have candidates with a variety of disabilities, possibly making it more challenging to identify neurodivergent candidates.

As shown in Figure 8.3, the sourcing partners discussed vary in their ability to target neurodivergent candidates with the necessary requirements to fit specific roles in your company. However, you may find working with several of these resources to be an effective way to develop a strong pipeline of neurodivergent talent.

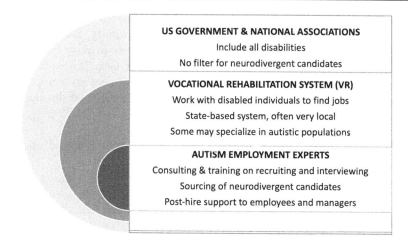

Figure 8.3 Targeting Autistic Candidates Through Sourcing Partners.

The Autism Community

As discussed in Chapter 7, the autism community extends beyond those with an ASD diagnosis, encompassing all of those related to or associated with someone on the spectrum. This includes not only family members and friends, but educators, coaches, therapists, and medical professionals who support autistic individuals. All these groups form their own communities to share resources and learn from each other about how to support themselves and their autistic family members, friends, and clients. The autism community can be found in support groups (live and online), on social media sites, and in clinical practices. Getting the word out to these groups about your autism hiring efforts, and how neurodivergent candidates can apply for roles in your organization, is critical to increasing your pipeline of autistic talent.

Support Groups

Peer support groups came into fashion in the US in the 1970s as part of a mental health consumer movement. Benefits of peer support groups include, among other things, improvements in patient outcomes, worksite wellness, productivity, and community outreach.[13] Today, one can find peer support groups in the autism community for individuals on the spectrum (oftentimes clustered by age ranges), for autistic women, for spouses/partners of autistic individuals, and for siblings and parents of children, teens, and adults on the spectrum. Groups also exist for autistics who identify as LGBTQIA+ and people of color. Many of these groups are coordinated and run by nonprofit organizations or autistic individuals.

Notifying support groups of available job openings in your organization is an effective way of increasing outreach into the community. Below is a sampling of organizations that either host support groups or provide listings of available support groups in their geography. A quick Google search of "autism support groups and [your location]" or "autism meet-up groups" generates many listings of local groups that can either be contacted through their websites or the group organizer.

- The Asperger/Autism Network (www.aane.org) – New England and New York
- Asperger/Autism Spectrum Education Network (www.aspennj.org) – New Jersey
- The Autism Services, Education, Resources, and Training Collaborative (www.paautism.org) – Pennsylvania
- Autism Asperger Spectrum Coalition for Education, Networking and Development (www.aascend.org) – Northern California
- Center for Autism and Related Disabilities (www. florida-card.org/map .htm) – Florida
- Global and Regional Asperger Syndrome Partnership (www.grasp.org) – Nationwide
- Interagency Work Group on Autism (https://iwg-autism.org/map) – Ohio

Clinical Practices

The therapeutic services needed to support autistic individuals are varied and can be many over the course of an individual's life. Professionals who serve the autism community include psychologists, neuropsychologists, psychiatrists, educators, social workers, life skills coaches, job coaches, occupational therapists, and speech and language therapists. These professionals can be a good source of job candidates, as they know their clients' work readiness capabilities and can be available to provide additional support to both the individual and employer, allowing for a more successful transition of the candidate into the workplace.

As most of these professionals are sole practitioners and work with a client base that is broader than just those on the autism spectrum, it is not always easy to identify them. There are ways, however, to seek out professionals who would be the most likely ones to be working in the field of autism. A couple of programs exist that certify professionals in treating autistic individuals. Seek out professionals who are working in or have gone through these training programs – two are listed below:

- The Asperger/Autism Network: AANE offers an AsperCoach training program and has certified life skills trainers throughout the country for adults with autism and Asperger Syndrome.

- Program for the Education and Enrichment of Relational Skills (PEERS®): This evidence-based social skills program for individuals with ASD and ADD/ADHD, anxiety, depression, and other socio-emotional problems was developed by University of California at Los Angeles and is now taught globally. Many major health systems in the US, particularly those at teaching universities, have a PEERS® program as part of their mental health services. Look for practitioners who are affiliated with those programs or have been trained in the PEERS® method.

Non-clinical professionals also serve the autism community. Special education lawyers and special needs financial planners work with autistic clients and their families on a regular basis and could also be a good source of potential referrals.

Social Media Sites

Just as you should be using your company's social media sites to communicate your neurodiversity hiring objectives to the autism community, you should be using social media sites favored by autistic individuals and their family and friends to learn about and reach the same audience. Facebook, Instagram, TikTok, Meet Up, and Twitter, among others, all have numerous individuals and groups dedicated to autism and neurodiversity. Use the search features to find appropriate groups and share your hiring objectives and open positions.

Conclusion

Any targeted hiring initiative is only successful if you can identify and recruit qualified candidates. It can be a struggle for some employers looking to employ autistic talent to find those candidates because they typically do not make it through the traditional recruiting process. Therefore, to find these candidates, employers need to think about using traditional recruiting sources in non-traditional ways and looking at some other avenues for finding talent. Thinking differently about how you use campus recruiting and the internet, utilizing the specialized sourcing partners available to help, and tapping into the autism community will help you build your pipeline of autistic jobseekers.

Notes

1 Annabi, Hala, E. W. Crooks, Neil Barnett, J. Guadagno, James R. Mahoney, J. Michelle, A. Pacilio, Hiren Shukla, and Jose Velasco. *Autism @ Work Playbook: Finding Talent and Creating Meaningful Employment Opportunities for People*

with Autism. Seattle, WA: ACCESS-IT, The Information School, University of Washington, 2019.

2 Cox, Bradley, Amanda Mintz, Taylor Locks, Kerry Thompson, Amelia Anderson, Lindee Morgan, Jeffrey Edelstein, and Abigail Wolz. "Academic Experiences for College Students with Autism: Identity, Disclosure, and Accommodations." 2015. http://myweb.fsu.edu/bcox2/_pdf/AERA2015paper.pdf.

3 College Autism Spectrum. "College Programs." September 19, 2020. http://collegeautismspectrum.com/collegeprograms/.

4 College Consultants. "Programs in College for Autism, Asperger, ADHD, LD, Neurodiversity." March 2, 2019. https://www.topcollegeconsultants.com/autism-in-college/.

5 McDermott, Catherine Tobin, and Brett Ranon Nachman. "United States College Programs for Autistic Students." *College Autism Network*, January 25, 2021. https://collegeautismnetwork.org/wp-content/uploads/2021/01/College-Autism-Specific-Support-Programs-1.25.2021.pdf.

6 Fisher, Julia Freeland. "How to Get a Job Often Comes Down to One Elite Personal Asset, and Many People Still Don't Realize It." *CNBC*, December 27, 2019. https://www.cnbc.com/2019/12/27/how-to-get-a-job-often-comes-down-to-one-elite-personal-asset.html.

7 Grund, Sandra. "What Every Job Seeker Should Know: Jobvite's 2020 Recruiter Nation Survey." *Jobvite*, October 13, 2020. https://www.jobvite.com/blog/hiring/what-every-job-seeker-should-know-jobvites-2020-recruiter-nation-survey/.

8 The Recruiter Network. "How Recruiters Effectively Use Social Media." *The Recruiter Network Blog* (blog). September 19, 2020. https://therecruiternetwork.com/blog/how-recruiters-effectively-use-social-media/.

9 GAO, General Accounting Office. "Vocational Rehabilitation: Additional Federal Information Could Help States Serve Employers and Find Jobs for People with Disabilities." *GAO-18-577*. Washington, DC, September 6, 2018, 14. https://www.gao.gov/assets/700/694369.pdf.

10 WRP. "Employers – Workforce Recruitment Program." September 19, 2020. https://www.wrp.gov/wrp?id=employer_landing_page.

11 AAAS. "'Entry Point!' American Association for the Advancement of Science." September 19, 2020. https://www.aaas.org/programs/entry-point.

12 AAPD. "Update on 2020 AAPD Summer Internship Program." *American Association of People with Disabilities*. September 19, 2020. https://www.aapd.com/press-releases/update-2020-summer-intern-program/.

13 Tang, Patrick. "A Brief History of Peer Support: Origins." *Peers for Progress*, June 7, 2013. http://peersforprogress.org/pfp_blog/a-brief-history-of-peer-support-origins/.

Part III

Interviewing

Chapter 9

The Autism Factor in Interviews

As humans, we are subject to first impressions, and currently the topic of *unconscious bias* is at the forefront of discussions about how companies hire and treat employees. It is hard to change human nature: even when someone's first impression is proven wrong by the introduction of new information, an implicit (or unconscious) bias may still exist. In the context of a job interview, unconscious bias, as discussed in Chapter 11, can disqualify perfectly good candidates. If a candidate's performance during an interview is contrary to the interviewer's initial impression, the interviewer may still not assess the candidate accurately due to that incorrect first impression.[1]

A survey of 2,000 hiring managers conducted in 2018 confirms the impact of first impressions. The survey found the following behaviors among interviewers:

- 33% knew if they would hire a candidate within 90 seconds of meeting them
- 65% did not hire candidates who did not make eye contact
- 50% would not consider a candidate based on how they dressed, acted, or walked through the door
- 40% felt lack of a smile was a good enough reason not to hire a candidate
- 40% eliminated a candidate based on the quality of their voice and overall confidence[2]

In order to make a "good" first impression in an interview, candidates are expected to dress for the role, display confident body language, make eye contact, smile, anticipate questions, and prepare answers relative to the role, as well as establish a connection with the interviewer. All these expectations require an individual to have strong social cognitive abilities, and as discussed in Chapter 4, autistic jobseekers may struggle in this area. In this chapter, we will discuss how the appearance, verbal acuity, and sensory sensitivities of autistic candidates may impact recruiter impressions in a job interview.

The Importance of Appearance

As the statistics above demonstrate, physical appearance plays a major role in the success of a person's job search. Autistic individuals may struggle making eye contact, maintaining their posture, or receiving and projecting appropriate facial expressions. They may also engage in repetitive body movements, such as fidgeting with a pen or rocking in their chair (see below for more on *stimming*) as a way to alleviate anxiety. Any of these ways of presenting can be a significant barrier to success in finding a job.

> Not all autistic individuals will present the same. No two individuals on the spectrum are affected by autism the same way, and the behaviors they demonstrate related to autism will be unique to them.

Look Me in the Eye

Eye contact is an important component of non-verbal communication. It plays a key role in how we interpret others' level of engagement and truthfulness in discussions. Not only do we rely on eye contact to determine if someone is interested in what we have to say or is telling the truth, but we also judge the way they make eye contact in determining their sincerity, confidence, and character. Many individuals on the spectrum will say "I can look at you or I can talk to you, but I can't do both at the same time". As this autistic professional explains:

> I've always struggled with eye contact … If somebody asks me a question and I'm engaged in thought, I'm working it through in my head, I typically look away … I think about the solution and then I will be able to answer the question.

Maintaining eye contact is not intuitive for some autistic individuals, while others have been taught rigorously from a young age to look people in the eye so that they stare intently at their discussion partner. It can be equally unsettling to interview someone who looks at you without blinking, resulting in a sense of anxiety or discomfort for the interviewer.

Noah Zandan, CEO of communication skills improvement platform Quantified Communications, estimates that adults typically make eye contact 30–60% of the time during daily conversation. However, communication coaches recommend the optimum amount of eye contact during an interview be somewhere between 60–90% of the time.[3] Even for neurotypical individuals, the amount of eye contact considered appropriate for an interview can be more than double what they are used to. This becomes another activity job candidates need to focus on during an interview to ensure they are making a good impression.

For some autistic candidates, making eye contact with an interviewer is just not an option, no matter how hard they try. A 2017 study conducted at Massachusetts General Hospital found that avoidance of eye contact in autistic individuals "is a way to decrease an unpleasant excessive arousal stemming from overactivation in a particular part of the brain".[4] In layman's terms, it can be physically painful for someone with autism to look others in the eye.

If you are interviewing a candidate who struggles with eye contact, do not jump to any conclusions as to why they are looking away. Continue to look at the candidate, as you would with any jobseeker, but also find opportunities to create an alternate focal point. Share the candidate's resume or the job description on paper or a computer screen and look together at specific line items you would like to discuss. Another option may be to sit side-by-side or take a walk with the candidate. These strategies are discussed further in Chapter 10.

Straighten Up

According to YAI, a national organization that provides services to people with disabilities, autistic individuals can have a "reduced perception of their body movement or shift relative to their own postural orientation and equilibrium".[5] This can affect how an individual walks, stands, or even sits. As a result, some autistic jobseekers may walk with a gait that seems odd or slouch when standing or sitting. This can also cause a disarrayed look in one's appearance, as poor posture can cause shirts to come untucked and clothes to become wrinkled.

If you notice that certain aspects of how a candidate walks into an interview or physically presents themselves are not consistent with what you would expect, it may be a sign of an autistic individual who is undisclosed. If you are interviewing a candidate who presents with posture issues, offer them a straight-backed chair, rather than a low, plush seat to sit in; and if the candidate appears messy upon arrival, offer them time to go to the restroom to "freshen up" before starting the interview. As a reminder, if you suspect a candidate is on the autism spectrum, do not inquire if this is the case. Please refer to Chapter 1 of this book for further discussion of disclosure.

Facial Expressions

Non-verbal communication through facial expressions is a two-way street. We learn a tremendous amount about what another person is trying to convey by watching their face, as well as telegraph our own thoughts, emotions, and reactions through facial expressions. As discussed in Chapter 4, processing social interactions can be a challenge for autistic individuals. Some people with autism struggle not only in reading the facial cues of others but their own facial expressions may not accurately reflect their emotions or may be entirely inappropriate for the situation at hand. We have met individuals who have told us, "When I am anxious, I smile, even if the situation is one that doesn't seem appropriate for smiling".

When interviewing autistic individuals, do not rely on non-verbal cues or facial expressions to convey information to the candidates. For example, if you are receiving too much information to a question, looking impatient or glancing at your watch will not necessarily register with the candidate that they should wrap up their answer. Politely interrupt the individual, let them know you've received the information you need, and move on to your next question. You may even give instructions for future questions, such as, "Please answer this for me in no more than three to four sentences". Not only does this provide the candidate with the direction they need, it will allow you to see whether the candidate can receive and follow instructions.

When a candidate's facial expression is either inappropriate for the discussion or provides no cues as to their inner thoughts, just remember that this is likely related to how autism affects them. If you are uncertain as to how a candidate is reacting to a question or situation, ask them to explain their reaction to you verbally. For example, at the end of an interview with a candidate who has not smiled, ask them if they find the role interesting and one they can see themselves in. Just because a candidate's face hasn't shown any outward signs of enthusiasm, it doesn't mean they aren't excited about the opportunity.

Repetitive Body Movements

Repetitive behaviors, also known as *stimming*, are one of the criteria used to determine if an individual qualifies for an autism diagnosis.[6] Stimming behaviors typically take the form of hand-flapping, pacing, body rocking, or fidgeting with objects.[7] They can also be in the form of a verbal vocalization, such as clearing one's throat. Some individuals will learn to "cloak" their stimming behaviors. According to an autistic professional in finance:

> For me flapping is a way of relieving stress and decompressing. I try to "cloak" it, and that's kind of masking what you're doing, by pretending I'm stretching.

Autistic individuals engage in stimming behaviors for a variety of reasons – to relieve anxiety or stress, as an expression of joy or happiness, or to maintain focus. Oftentimes the individual may not even be aware they are engaging in these behaviors, or that they may be distracting to others. Keep in mind that almost everyone engages in stimming behavior at times (drumming fingers during a meeting, biting nails, etc.), as evidenced by the popularity of stress balls and fidgets.

If you are interviewing a candidate who displays stimming behaviors, be aware that these are perfectly normal attributes of autistic individuals and have no impact on the candidate's ability to do a job. If the stimming seems to be increasing during the interview, ask the individual if they would like to take a break, in case the stimming is being caused by increasing levels of anxiety.

Ways of Speaking

Not only do job candidates need to be prepared to answer a variety of questions when going through the interview process, they need to do so in a clear and confident manner. The quality of an individual's voice and the way in which they deliver their answers make a strong impression on the interviewer, regardless of the content of what the candidate says. Therefore, autistic jobseekers who have differences in processing speed or vocal rhythm and intonation may be at a significant disadvantage.

The Long Pause

The ideal interview is a naturally flowing conversation: the interviewer asks a question, and the job candidate takes a second or two to gather their thoughts and then answers the question. A skilled interviewee may even paraphrase the question to gain a bit more time to formulate an answer. Some autistic and neurodivergent individuals experience processing speed differences,[8] requiring them to take additional time to listen to and formulate an answer to interview questions. This extra time, though possibly only seconds long, can seem interminable to a busy interviewer. Do not try to fill the silence. Remember that some autistic individuals are *deliberative thinkers*, as discussed in Chapter 11, so let the candidate finish thinking before answering the question.

If you find a candidate is taking long pauses and still struggles to understand and answer your questions, it may be in the phrasing of the questions. In Chapter 11 we discuss re-phrasing typical interview questions to help candidates who struggle with processing issues. Lastly, some autistic interviewees may repeat your question, in its entirety, every time, as a lead-in to their answer to your questions. This may be a strategy used to gain extra time to formulate their answer, rather than leaving an awkward silence, or a way of reinforcing the processing of the question for the candidate. While this may seem odd to you as the interviewer, it is not meant to mock the interviewer in any way, but simply to assist the individual in providing the best responses possible.

Everyone receives and processes information differently – autistic or not. For most people, learning comes through multiple forms – seeing (visually), hearing (auditory), and touching (kinesthetically or "hands-on"). Research has shown that autistic individuals are more likely to learn through one modality.[9] The typical interview process is heavily dependent on an individual's verbal (auditory) processing skills. This puts those who are visual and/or kinesthetic learners at a disadvantage.

Studies show that people with autism excel at visual learning.[10] Once again, if you find a candidate is taking long pauses and still struggles to understand and answer your questions after you have rephrased them, you may be dealing with a visual learner who needs to process the information in a different format. Chapter 10 discusses non-traditional interview formats that might better suit this type of candidate.

Vocal Prosody

Vocal prosody is the "rhythm, stress, and intonation of speech"[11] that provides us with a significant amount of information beyond the actual words of the speaker. Some autistic individuals have an unusual vocal prosody, the most common being a monotone or sing-song type of delivery. As with facial expressions, it is important to listen carefully to the content of the candidate's words and not become distracted by an atypical vocal prosody. The individual cannot control this aspect of their presentation and is not telegraphing any particular emotions or underlying thoughts as a result.

Turn Down the Volume

We have all had the experience of being in a noisy environment – a cocktail party, a stadium, a train station – while trying to engage in conversation with someone. In order to hear our discussion partner, our brain engages in a process called *sensory gating*.[12] This process takes place in the brain and allows us to block out irrelevant stimuli so we can focus on what is being said. Not surprisingly, given their neurological differences, autistic individuals often experience extreme responses to sound, light, smell, or touch. In effect, their sensory gating does not work in many situations. This can prove challenging in interview settings where multiple distractions (that may not be apparent to the interviewer) are bombarding the senses of the candidate. For a more detailed discussion of *sensory sensitivities*, see Chapter 4.

Interviewing on its own can be an anxiety-inducing experience; however, when autistic individuals' senses are overwhelmed, they experience *sensory overload*, which typically results in an even greater increase in anxiety. Being mindful of the sensory aspects of your office environment allows the candidate to perform to the best of their ability.

For candidates who are disclosed, ask them which, if any, sensory sensitivities they experience. Regardless of knowing if a candidate is on the spectrum, hold interviews in private spaces away from copy rooms, pantries and cafeterias, gathering spaces, high-traffic hallways, and other employees. Seat the candidate so they are facing you and not looking out at a busy exterior environment. If your computer screen is visible, turn it off, unless you plan on using it during the interview. If your space has harsh fluorescent lighting, ask candidates if they would like the lights lowered or turned off, if possible. If a candidate struggles with touch and has a poor handshake, or declines to shake hands, let it pass.

The world of remote work and interviewing has changed the interview experience for many recruiters, hiring managers, and candidates. Yet, the issues related to distraction still apply when interviewing autistic jobseekers remotely. Make sure your background environment is clean and professional. Do not have pets, family members, or roommates appearing on screen. Turn off landlines and cell phones that might ring during your interview. Center your camera so your full face is visible and check your lighting to avoid shadows.

Conclusion

Neurological differences related to autism may cause autistic jobseekers to present differently in interviews. However, human nature causes us to make judgments about others based on first impressions, making it difficult for many on the spectrum to make it past a first interview. Understanding challenges related to eye contact, facial expressions, processing speeds, learning styles, and sensory overload will allow employers to provide an interview experience that reduces autistic candidates' anxiety and allows them to demonstrate their talents to the best of their ability.

Notes

1 Okten, Irmak Olcaysoy. "Studying First Impressions: What to Consider?" *APS Observer* 31, no. 2 (January 31, 2018). https://www.psychologicalscience.org/observer/studying-first-impressions-what-to-consider.

2 Twin Group. "8 Surprising Statistics about Interviews." *Twin Employment & Training*, March 2018. https://www.twinemployment.com/blog/8-surprising-statistics-about-interviews.

3 McKeever, Vicky. "How Much Eye Contact Is Too Much in a Job Interview?" *CNBC*, March 12, 2020. https://www.cnbc.com/2020/03/11/how-much-eye-contact-is-too-much-in-a-job-interview.html.

4 Massachusetts General Hospital. "Why Do Those with Autism Avoid Eye Contact? Imaging Studies Reveal Overactivation of Subcortical Brain Structures in Response to Direct Gaze." *ScienceDaily*, October 7, 2020. www.sciencedaily.com/releases/2017/06/170615213252.htm.

5 Zwick, Dalia. "Posture and Gait in Individuals with Autism Spectrum Disorder (ASD)." November 12, 2020. https://www.yai.org/news-stories/blog/posture-and-gait-individuals-autism-spectrum-disorder-asd.

6 CDC. "Diagnostic Criteria for Autism Spectrum Disorder (ASD)." *Centers for Disease Control and Prevention*, June 29, 2020. https://www.cdc.gov/ncbddd/autism/hcp-dsm.html.

7 Deweert, Sarah. "Repetitive Behaviors and 'Stimming' in Autism, Explained." *Spectrum Autism Research News* (blog), January 31, 2020. https://www.spectrumnews.org/news/repetitive-behaviors-and-stimming-in-autism-explained/.

8 Haigh, Sarah M., Jennifer A. Walsh, Carla A. Mazefsky, Nancy J. Minshew, and Shaun M. Eack. "Processing Speed Is Impaired in Adults with Autism Spectrum Disorder, and Relates to Social Communication Abilities." *Journal of Autism and Developmental Disorders* 48, no. 8 (August 2018): 2653. https://doi.org/10.1007/s10803-018-3515-z.

9 Edelson, Stephen M. "Learning Styles & Autism." *Autism Research Institute* (blog). October 7, 2020. https://www.autism.org/learning-styles-autism/.

10 Deweert, Sarah. "Attention to Detail May Aid Visual Learning in Autism." *Spectrum Autism Research News* (blog), September 23, 2014. https://www.spectrumnews.org/opinion/attention-to-detail-may-aid-visual-learning-in-autism/.

11 APA. "Prosody in Speech and Song." *American Psychological Association*, September 11, 2014. https://www.apa.org/pubs/highlights/peeps/issue-29#.

12 Lloyd-Thomas, Peter. "Sensory Gating in Autism, Particularly Asperger's." *Epiphany* (blog), March 26, 2017. https://epiphanyasd.blogspot.com/2017/03/sensory-gating-in-autism-particularly.html.

Chapter 10

Interview Alternatives

According to career coach and author Orville Pierson, the average jobseeker will need to receive 24 rejections from hiring decision-makers before receiving just one job offer.[1] Prior to meeting any one of those decision-makers, however, there are multiple points in the interview process where a candidate can be eliminated. Figure 10.1 shows what we call the "interview funnel". Most candidates need to pass successfully through each level of this funnel before receiving the coveted job offer.

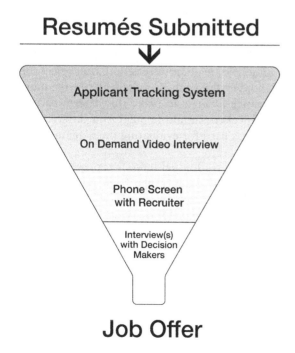

Figure 10.1 The "Interview Funnel" for Job Candidates.

As a result, interviewing can often seem like a test of one's endurance skills, akin to running a marathon, rather than one's job skills. As can be seen from the interview funnel, the process includes a number of hurdles, any of which can result in a candidate being "kicked out".

Interviewing is anxiety producing for even the most social of individuals; in fact, 93% of people report experiencing anxiety when going for a job interview.[2] However, most jobseekers develop strategies for managing this anxiety, allowing them to push through the process until they secure a position. For autistic individuals who experience social communication challenges, the traditional interview process can produce debilitating levels of anxiety, causing them to perform poorly or opt out altogether. This chapter discusses non-traditional interview formats that are less anxiety provoking, with a focus on an assessment of the skills necessary for the job and providing autistic jobseekers the opportunity to demonstrate their value to employers.

Non-traditional Formats

Companies conduct interviews to assess both the skill set and cultural fit of jobseekers for positions they need to fill. To determine that fit, most interviewers ask questions to determine a candidate's credentials, their motivations, and the influence of past behaviors on future behavior. To be successful in this type of interview, the candidate needs to understand the interviewer's underlying goals in asking the questions and be comfortable engaging in conversation with strangers. For autistic individuals who often have challenges related to theory of mind and social communication, the traditional interview can be a minefield, leading to rejection after rejection. To assess the fit of an autistic candidate for a job, recruiters and hiring managers may need to employ alternative formats to make this determination. This is not to say that autistic jobseekers should be held to a different, or lesser, standard, but that the methods used for evaluating them against that standard should be flexible.

There are several ways in which the traditional interview process can be modified to suit autistic individuals. These can range from minor adjustments to existing interview practices to creating an entirely separate process for autistic candidates. As practitioners in the field, we typically recommend employers begin with slight modifications to their existing interview practices, such as having no more than two interviewers meet with a candidate at one time and having no more than two interviews in a day, customizing the modifications to address each individual's needs. Most autistic jobseekers seeking professional-level roles will be aware of the adjustments that will allow them to navigate the interview process successfully. As an employer, offering a menu of options to candidates will allow them to request what they need without placing them in the position of having to raise the issue with you first, potentially obviating the need for disclosure.

Regardless of how you choose to adjust your interview practices to support autistic jobseekers, remember to preview the interview process for candidates. This affords them the opportunity to ask for accommodations and minimize their anxiety. For additional information on the importance of previewing, refer to Chapter 5.

Interview Practice Modifications

The typical interview consists of a conversation between two people sitting across from each other. One of the key features of this interaction is good eye contact. As discussed in Chapter 9, for individuals who struggle maintaining eye contact, this can make it near impossible for them to answer questions and properly convey their abilities to an interviewer.

Walk and Talk

For autistic jobseekers who struggle with eye contact, arranging the interview environment so it doesn't have a face-to-face setup may be all that is needed to facilitate conversation. If you see a candidate is looking away and struggling to answer your questions, suggest the two of you take a walk and continue your conversation while walking. We call this the *walk and talk* interview. When you know beforehand that a candidate is uncomfortable making eye contact, have a seating arrangement where you sit side-by-side at a table or desk, with the candidate's resume on the table surface as a focal point for the two of you to discuss.

Show and Tell

In addition to the *walk and talk*, another interview modification is what we call *show and tell*. As discussed in Chapter 9, some autistic individuals are visual and/or kinesthetic learners. They might struggle to explain to an interviewer how to *hypothetically* tackle a problem but can be more comfortable *showing* the interviewer what they know. For example, a candidate who cannot *describe* to you how he would create a pivot table in Excel may *demonstrate* that skill when presented with a laptop and asked to do so. If you are interviewing an individual who is struggling to answer questions that can be answered by showing you how they would approach the problem you are posing, provide them with the tools to do so. This could range from having a candidate write an example down on paper to sketching a problem or design out on a white board or using relevant computer software or a search engine to find the answer to your question.

Single vs. Panel Interviews

Not all interviews are conducted as one-on-one discussions. Many employers use panels, consisting of multiple interviewers, to meet with a candidate.

This is done to use everyone's time efficiently and reduce bias, as each interviewer will have the same experience with the candidate. For autistic individuals, meeting with more than one person at a time can be extremely anxiety provoking. If this is your practice, ask candidates if they have a preference to meet with just one interviewer at a time or are comfortable meeting with multiple people at once. Some individuals may be comfortable meeting with two people but draw the limit at three. Other candidates may be fine with more than one person in the interview but prefer to have one of those individuals designated as the primary interviewer who asks the questions, so they can maintain focus. If a candidate expresses a preference, make sure you honor their request. Ensuring that additional individuals have a chance to meet or observe the candidate can also be accomplished by using video technology for the interview: consider recording it for some of the interviewers to watch after the fact. Just remember to get the candidate's permission to record and share the interview.

Super Days vs. Separate Days

One of the biggest tests of any jobseeker's endurance capabilities is what some companies call "super" days. On super days, companies will have candidates come in for a full day of interviews, consisting of up to six or seven back-to-back meetings, plus lunch with a group of employees. While some autistic candidates will be fine with this format, many will struggle to make it through the day. Experiencing a sustained level of anxiety will result in most autistic individuals being unable to maintain the energy needed: by midday, many of these candidates will no longer be able to demonstrate their best selves. Rather than having autistic individuals participate in super days, offer them the alternative of splitting their interview sessions into two or three separate days, without lunch. Some individuals on the spectrum are sensitive to smells or have aversion to specific foods and will find it difficult to have to eat with a group of strangers. Others may be fine with a full day of interviews but need the lunch break time alone to recharge for the afternoon.

Technical Skills Reviews

Like the *show and tell* modification described above, a traditional question-and-answer interview may reveal less about a candidate's ability to meet the job requirements than an interview process where the candidate "shows" you what they can do. For autistic individuals, particularly those with specific technical skills (including but not limited to computer programming, coding, accounting, graphic design, data analysis, technical writing, and editing), a skills-based interview format may provide the interviewer with a better insight into the candidate's abilities and the candidate with a better format for demonstrating their skills.

This type of interview can be adapted to many types of roles. At Integrate, we test the capabilities of candidates (autistic or not) for a program manager role by asking them to:

1. Create a graph in PowerPoint using a data set provided in Excel
2. Complete a mail merge and print a properly formatted thank you note to a donor in Word
3. Write a two to three paragraph summary of research conducted on a topic of the candidate's choice related to autism

These tests were designed to evaluate the candidate's familiarity with the Microsoft Office skills required for the role, as well as the individual's general writing and research skills. Table 10.1 lists other examples our clients have used for various roles.

Table 10.1 Sample Skills Assessments for Various Roles

Role	Sample Demonstration of Skills
Multimedia Intern	Creation of a static graphic and a GIF that include the company's logo, formatted for three different social media sites
Staff Accountant	Problems requiring the analysis of an income statement and balance sheet, determining journal entries, and calculating depreciation
Software Engineer	Coding exercise

As mentioned previously, some candidates may not be able to convey their skill sets as effectively in the question-and-answer format employers are accustomed to. We recommend to our hiring clients that they provide technical skills tests to autistic candidates *before* conducting a more traditional interview. Our goal in doing this is to favorably dispose the interviewers to the candidates who demonstrate the skills necessary for the role prior to conducting the more traditional interview, as these may not necessarily be the candidates who do best in the traditional interview format.

Customized or Separate Interview Process

Some organizations have set up autism hiring programs that include a customized interview process for candidates – separate from their traditional interview practices and processes. This approach is often a one- to multi-week program. Most employers that take such an approach require autistic jobseekers to take a technical skills test before accepting them into the program. Once a candidate is accepted into the program, they join a group of other neurodivergent applicants at the employer's offices. During the program, the applicants may have the opportunity to engage in the following:

- Team projects and team-building exercises – typically observed by hiring managers
- Workplace skills/readiness training
- Informal meetings to socialize with hiring managers, recruiters, current neurodivergent employees, and other applicants
- Practice interviews with feedback
- Interviews with hiring managers

If an employer runs this program for several weeks, candidates typically work on longer-term projects and get paid. Once the program is completed, the employer determines which candidates will receive an offer of employment.

Over time, we have seen most companies that use this interviewing format move to a shorter, one- to two-week, program. While this separate interview process may be well-suited to some individuals on the autism spectrum, it is important to remember that it will limit access to candidates who cannot relocate for one or more weeks, thereby reducing overall access to potential candidates for the employer.

A Word about Virtual Interviewing

The use of technology for interviewing is becoming more common. The COVID-19 pandemic has accelerated this movement, with 86% of employers saying they have incorporated virtual technologies as part of their interview process. It is expected that these new technologies will be the standard, even post-pandemic.[3] When using technology platforms to screen autistic candidates, it is equally important to consider adjustments that may be needed to ensure a smooth interviewing experience. Below are some suggestions to create an autism-friendly experience for your candidates:

- Provide clear instructions on the technology platform you will be using, including links to any software the candidate may need to download and/or accounts they may need to create prior to the interview (e.g., Zoom, Microsoft Teams, Webex, Skype, etc.).
- Offer a test session with the candidate, prior to the scheduled interview date, to confirm the technology is working properly.
- Make sure any virtual backgrounds being used by your interviewers are not visually distracting or do not cause the interviewer's image to fade in and out from the screen.
- Instruct your interviewers to have no distractions (i.e., pets, other household members) entering the field of vision of the screen during an interview.
- If you are using an on-demand interview platform requiring timed responses, make it clear that candidates do not have to use the entire time allotted unless they wish to do so.

- If you are using an on-demand platform with timed responses and a countdown clock is on the screen, be aware that this can cause undue anxiety for autistic individuals, causing them to struggle answering the questions. Be prepared to offer some form of accommodation, such as eliminating the time restriction, if possible. (See Chapter 11 for a further discussion of on-demand interview platforms.)

The Interview Process: A Different Perspective

When looking to hire autistic individuals, it is important to remember what you are trying to achieve throughout your interview process. The interview process typically serves to winnow down a large applicant pool to a few qualified candidates. For large employers, that process often starts with eliminating many applicants through an automated resume review process. It may next involve screening out candidates by having them conduct an on-demand interview using one of the many virtual interviewing platforms that exist. Then a candidate may have a phone screen (or phone interview) with a recruiter before moving on to discussions with one or more hiring managers. The goal of the process is to identify a select group of qualified candidates using the time of recruiters and hiring managers as efficiently as possible.

For neurodiversity hiring programs, however, the interview process should be about increasing your applicant pool and creating a process that supports qualified candidates through to an offer. This requires a different perspective in designing the interview process. Rather than relying on a low-touch process – one that depends heavily on screens by automated resume review systems and virtual interviewing platforms – it is necessary to incorporate manual interventions into these processes so that qualified candidates do not get screened out. Some of these manual interventions can include:

- Providing candidates with a contact through your applicant tracking system to disclose their disability at the time they apply, if they wish, or a link to an alternate site expressly for neurodivergent individuals. This should automatically result in a trained recruiter reviewing the resume in addition to the automated system review.
- Programming your applicant tracking system to identify and highlight resumes of candidates who have indicated participation in a predetermined list of autism support college programs or other autism-related programs.
- Reviewing candidates who score low on your virtual interviewing platform but have resumes that indicate they may be well-suited to the role(s) you are looking to fill. These candidates may struggle with anxiety or present with verbal processing differences or delays or have non-typical cognitive styles that can result in low scores on the on-demand video

interviews. Yet they may possess all the skills required to do the job and excel when offered some of the interview modifications discussed above.

Identifying neurodivergent candidates as they go through the interview process is an important step, no matter how that interview process is designed. It is equally important that everyone involved, from recruiters to hiring managers, have a level of awareness about how these candidates may present and how to best interview them. Train your interviewers on how to interview neurodivergent candidates effectively. Many of the autism employment experts referred to in Chapter 8 offer such training in live and webinar formats. Companies, such as Uptimize, offer video platforms that include modules on interviewing neurodivergent talent. Chapter 11 provides guidance on how to phrase interview questions for maximum effect with autistic candidates.

Conclusion

Employers need to approach the interview process for autistic talent as one of *inclusion* rather than a process of exclusion, eliminating the hurdles that are typically used to screen large applicant pools. The traditional interview process is a barrier to entry to the work world for many autistic individuals; while they may have the skill sets to do the job, they typically struggle with the social communication skills needed to succeed in interviews.

Employers can modify their interview process in several ways, from making minor adjustments to existing practices to developing a customized or separate process, creating a level playing field for autistic jobseekers. The goal, however, is to hold *all* candidates to an equal standard of performance, while providing autistic jobseekers the flexibility they need to successfully go through the interview process.

Notes

1 Kudisch, Jeffrey. "Turned Down for a Job? You Are Now One Rejection Closer to Success." *Los Angeles Times*, March 17, 2017. https://www.latimes.com/business/la-fi-career-coach-job-rejection-20170317-story.html.
2 JDP. "New Study Reveals How Americans Prepare for Job Interviews in 2020." April 30, 2020. https://www.jdp.com/blog/how-to-prepare-for-interviews-2020/.
3 Gartner. "Gartner HR Survey Shows 86% of Organizations Are Conducting Virtual Interviews to Hire Candidates During Coronavirus Pandemic." *Gartner*, April 20, 2020. https://www.gartner.com/en/newsroom/press-releases/2020-04-30-gartner-hr-survey-shows-86--of-organizations-are-cond.

Chapter 11

What Are You Evaluating?

Mindset Versus Skill Set

Modern recruiting practices entail more than marking off a checklist of skills and keywords, and the deciding factor in someone's candidacy often involves more subjective assessments of motivation, soft skills, and organizational fit. The emphasis on candidates having the right attitude, or "mindset", can be deemed just as important as possessing the right skills for a position, which often presents difficulties for autistic jobseekers.

This chapter will explore issues of mindset and skill set relating to interview questions, as well as the development and adoption of new technologies to further a more scientific approach to recruiting.

Mindset

One can Google "the best interview questions" and find hundreds of websites and blogs with the top ten, 15, and 20 lists of best interview questions to ask candidates. If you take the time to read through a number of these sites, you will begin to see a pattern. These questions are intended to evaluate a candidate's *mindset*, which according to Merriam-Webster dictionary is (1) a mental attitude or inclination or (2) a fixed state of mind.[1] In recruiting, mindset tends to specifically refer to a "growth" mindset versus a "fixed" mindset, a concept developed further by Stanford University psychologist Carol Dweck, who identifies those with a *growth mindset* as individuals who believe in lifelong learning, embrace challenge, and learn from criticism.[2] Dr. Dweck says those with a *fixed mindset* tend to believe their talents are innate and will not change, resulting in a tendency to avoid challenges and a dislike of negative feedback.

Take a typical interview question, such as "Tell me about a professional failure you've experienced". Someone with a fixed mindset might struggle to come up with a time they failed or say they never have. A candidate with a growth mindset, however, will likely explain what happened, the lesson(s) learned from the situation, and how he/she would act differently in the future.[3]

It was never Dr. Dweck's thesis that growth and fixed mindset exist exclusively of one another. Indeed, she acknowledges that "we all have our own fixed mindset triggers ... and that we must all identify and work with these triggers".[4] Yet a quick Google search for "interviewing for growth mindset" yields articles with quotes like these:

- "Someone with a growth mindset believes that skill development and talent are derivatives of personal will and effort. Conversely, the *evil counterpart* [emphasis added] of the growth mindset is the fixed mindset, which believes that success is a personally defining label".[5]
- "Where fixed mindset candidates focus on the possibility of rejection, growth mindset candidates focus on the upside. Where fixed mindset candidates wing it and cross their fingers, growth mindset candidates know they can win most any position with practiced skills in the interview room. Where fixed mindset candidates see roadblocks, growth mindset candidates see hurdles".[6]

Given the positive spin put on growth mindsets, contemporary advice for recruiters oftentimes sounds more like Darwinian advice on how to use the interview process to weed out those with a fixed mindset. More importantly, this false dichotomy fails to account for the unique cognitive style of candidates with neurodivergent profiles and discourages following a process that allows one to determine whether a candidate can successfully do the job. For autistic jobseekers, particularly those who may not disclose during an interview process, being perceived by an interviewer as someone with a fixed mindset, whether consciously or not, is oftentimes a significant obstacle in obtaining employment.

Mindset of the Autistic Candidate

Two concepts are important to understand when evaluating an autistic candidate's mindset – theory of mind and thinking style. As discussed in Chapter 4, theory of mind is the ability we develop somewhere between the ages of three to five to understand the thoughts, desires, perspectives, and beliefs of others, without necessarily having to be told. It is commonly referred to as "putting yourself in someone else's shoes", and in the workplace is a key element for understanding the social and work-related needs of others. Many autistic individuals will have some challenges, from moderate to severe, with theory of mind. This puts them at a disadvantage in an interview setting relative to their neurotypical peers, who intuitively know that interviewers are often seeking more nuanced, less-obvious answers to some questions.

Thinking Styles

Everyone's thinking style manifests in multiple ways and has a significant impact on how we are perceived by others. Some individuals who struggle with theory of mind are also literal thinkers. They view the world in terms of "black and white" and "right and wrong" and may come across as rigid thinkers. As you can imagine, such an individual might present as someone with a fixed mindset, despite being a lifelong learner and gaining considerable expertise in their subject matter of choice. Therefore, it is important to ask interview questions in a clear and direct manner, providing candidates with opportunities to demonstrate their mindset and skill sets in multiple ways.

Another type of thinking is *intuitive* versus *deliberative*. There are times when our physical and psychological survival depends on our reacting quickly and automatically, such as avoiding a car that jumped the light or interpreting the facial expression of an angry supervisor. On the other hand, when making a complex decision our thinking tends to be slower and more analytical. In *Thinking Fast and Slow,* psychologist/economist and Nobel laureate Daniel Kahneman, known for his work on the psychology of judgment and decision-making, describes how these two modes of thinking and making decisions work together.[7] *Intuition* and fast thinking is a "big picture" process that uses mental shortcuts based on experience and limited information to make decisions; however, this can lead to jumping to conclusions and be prone to errors. *Deliberative* thinking, on the other hand, is slow, controlled, and effortful, as it requires attending to the details required to wrestle with difficult problems. Consequently, we tend to use deliberation only when necessary and use our intuition as a shortcut for everyday decisions, even though it may sometimes not be accurate.

Autistic individuals are known for their focus on detail, which can sometimes lead them to miss the "big picture", particularly in the workplace.[8] Recent research on the thinking styles of individuals with autism suggests that they are not "lazy thinkers" and instead tend to rely on deliberation (even in everyday decisions). As a result, they are less likely to respond intuitively during logical reasoning and decision-making.[9] This can have negative consequences during a job interview, where answering questions after long deliberation can give the wrong impression.

Cognitive Bias

As humans, we often make quick decisions based on intuition, and how we think is often influenced by various unconscious biases – cognitive shortcuts that feed into our decision-making and judgments, such as stereotyping and the tendency to weigh the latest information more heavily than older data.[10] Recruiters are often told to "trust your gut" which can result in unconscious hiring bias.[11] In fact, research suggests that when making hiring decisions, people tend to value someone with "natural talent" over "strivers", even when they claim to value motivation, hard work, and perseverance.[12]

For autistic individuals, challenges with theory of mind and differences in thinking styles, when compared to their neurotypical peers, may be interpreted by others as a fixed mindset. However, this does not account for their history of perseverance in a world biased toward neurotypicals, their tendency to become subject matter experts, and their dogged determination to work at a problem until it is solved – which in this context, we believe, is more indicative of a growth mindset.

The Deliberative Mindset

The study of mindsets continues, as evidenced by the recent identification of a "strategic mindset", the tendency to ask one's self the following questions when approaching a challenging goal or experiencing a setback: "How might I go about this differently? Is there another approach I can try to help this go better?"[13] As these studies primarily focus on neurotypical subjects, we would like to include an additional mindset that more accurately captures the thought processes of autistic individuals we have observed, and accounts for the autistic's reliance on more deliberative thinking over intuition: the *deliberative mindset*.

Researchers refer to the deliberative mindset as a lens that encourages individuals to deliberatively consider multiple angles, leading to more unbiased processing of information, increased critical thinking, and improved judgments.[14] Viewed in this light, a deliberative mindset is not seen as inherently negative, but instead reveals specific attributes associated with a style of thinking that may be considered an asset in certain job roles. Table 11.1 compares the growth and fixed mindsets with the deliberative mindset.

Table 11.1 Comparison of Growth, Fixed, and Deliberative Mindsets

	Growth Mindset	Fixed Mindset	Deliberative Mindset
Skills	Developed from hard work and always improving	Ability is innate and considers knowledge complete	Narrowly focused but always learning
Challenges	Embraces them as opportunities for growth	Avoids them and gives up easily	Focuses on overcoming select challenges
Effort	Considered essential and enjoys the journey	Considered unnecessary if one is qualified	Considers focus and persistence necessary for problem-solving
Feedback	Finds it useful and learns from it	Feels it's unwarranted and takes it personally	Welcome and respected from trusted individuals
Setbacks	Considers a wakeup call to do better	Blames others and gives up	Persists till the problem is solved

Interview Questions

Experts will tell you anywhere from three to eight different types of interview questions exist. In our experience, interview questions fall into five basic categories. As can be seen in Table 11.2, these categories of questions can run the gamut from straightforward to bewildering, such as, "If you could be any part of a bicycle, what part would you be?"

For autistic jobseekers, credentials and experience questions, when phrased clearly, are easily answered. These questions are fact-based, requiring candidates to recount actual personal experiences. An interviewer should expect to get clear, direct answers from autistic individuals to these questions, given their tendency towards honesty and logical thought.

For individuals who present as job-hoppers, experience questions are a good tool to use to uncover the nature of their frequent job moves. It is completely appropriate to ask a candidate, "Why did you leave your position at XYZ company?" or to say, "I see you have held a number of different jobs during the past few years. Can you tell me the circumstances under which you left each position?" As discussed in Chapter 6, it will often be the case that autistic individuals who have held multiple, short-term positions were not disclosed to their prior employers or worked in environments that were not supportive of neurodivergent individuals. Once you have gained some insight into the reasons a candidate has left prior positions, you can follow up with behavioral questions related to the situations the individual encountered to learn more about them. Be aware, however, it is when faced with behavioral, opinion, and brain-teaser questions that autistic jobseekers may begin to struggle. As a result, interviewers might see them as candidates with a fixed mindset – rigid, fearful, and negative.

Table 11.2 Types of Interview Questions

Type of Question	Goal of Question	Sample Question
Credentials	Factual information	What was your GPA in college?
Experience	Evaluate technical knowledge/ skills	What were your responsibilities in your last position?
Behavioral	Predictor of future behavior based on past behaviors	Tell me about a time you had to resolve a conflict with a co-worker.
Opinion	Predictor of future behavior based on personal views	What is your greatest weakness?
Brain-teaser	Test ability to think	How many jellybeans are in that jar on my desk?

Issues with Behavioral, Opinion, and Brain-Teaser Questions

Let's start with behavioral and opinion questions. Two issues can arise for autistic candidates with these types of questions. First, how the interviewer phrases the question can make the difference between the candidate being able to answer the question or not. Oftentimes behavioral and opinion questions require the interviewee to offer their views on what another person might be thinking or about a situation. Recalling the discussion of theory of mind earlier in this chapter, the act of "putting oneself in the position of another" can be a major challenge for autistic individuals. For example, while screening an autistic candidate for a position, we asked him the following typical opinion question, "If I spoke to your supervisor, what would she tell me is your greatest strength?" His perfectly logical response for someone who struggles with theory of mind was, "I don't know. You'd have to ask my supervisor". In this instance, we asked the candidate to "put himself in the mind of his supervisor" which, given his challenges with theory of mind, he could not do. However, by slightly rephrasing the question to "If I spoke to your supervisor, what *do you think* she would tell me is your greatest strength?" he had no trouble answering the question, because we asked him for *his own* opinion, rather than that of his supervisor.

Second, many autistic jobseekers experience significant rejection in their job search process. Due to their social communication challenges, they usually spend much longer looking for a job, as these challenges become a barrier to entry to the workforce. As a result, autistic candidates, particularly those who overshare (see our companion book, *An Employer's Guide to Managing Professionals on the Autism Spectrum*), tend to focus on their negative experiences. In response to a behavioral question such as "Tell me about a time you had a conflict with a teammate about a project at work and how it was resolved", an autistic candidate might go on at length about their difficulties with their teammate, rather than quickly tell you about the conflict, what they did to fix the situation, and what they learned from the experience.

Candidates with social communication struggles may also perseverate – or hold onto – negative events in their lives, making it difficult for them to see the lessons learned from these experiences or at least recognize the importance of only briefly mentioning them during an interview and focusing on the positive outcome(s). Lastly, individuals who are deliberative thinkers may pause for what seems to be an uncomfortably long period of time while they process the various conflict scenarios they've experienced to make sure they choose just the right one to recount.[15] This extra time, which in reality may only be two or three seconds, can feel like an extremely long and awkward silence in the context of an interview, particularly if the interviewer is unaware of the candidate's thinking or processing style.

Brain-teaser questions pose a similar challenge, as the interviewer is expecting the candidate to understand – or intuit – the hidden meaning of a question and answer accordingly. For example, autistic individuals who are literal thinkers, and struggle with theory of mind and seeing the big picture, may not figure out that when the interviewer points to a jar of jellybeans on their desk and asks, "How many jellybeans are in that jar?", the interviewer wants the candidate to provide the formula for determining the volume of the jar and then give an estimate based on the size of the jellybeans. An autistic candidate is as likely to answer, "I don't know, I need to count them" or "That's a stupid question".

Interviewers use behavioral, opinion, and brain-teaser questions as proxies to predict how candidates might perform on some aspect of a job if hired. It is interesting to note that Google abandoned brain-teaser questions after an analysis of thousands of the company's hiring decisions showed no correlation between successful answers to such questions and future job performance.[16] To screen for problem-solving, a question more predictive of how someone will perform might be "Describe for me a hard problem you solved in your XYZ class at school or at your last job and how you went about solving it", allowing the interviewer to then drill down for specific examples.

Rephrasing Interview Questions

Given that autistic candidates may struggle with behavioral, opinion, and brain-teaser questions, you might be wondering how you can test for possible performance on the job in certain areas. Worded appropriately, all these categories of questions can be used effectively in interviews with autistic candidates. One could even argue that all candidates would benefit from a rethink of how these questions are presented. For autistic candidates, the key elements in phrasing questions are (1) clarity and (2) asking questions in relation to the candidate's own experiences/thought processes, rather than asking them to describe someone else's experiences/thought processes. Limiting the scope of brain-teasers keeps people who are more deliberative thinkers and have difficulty seeing the "big picture" from getting lost in the details.

Table 11.3 provides some examples of behavioral, opinion, and brain-teaser questions which have been rephrased for neurodivergent candidates.

Example 11.1 in the Appendix at the end of the book provides rephrased examples of typical credentials, experience, behavioral and opinion interview questions. The unifying feature between the rephrasing of all these questions is additional clarification of what the interviewer is seeking from the candidate, reducing their reliance on intuitive thinking.

Not all autistic individuals will present the same. No two individuals on the spectrum are affected by autism the same way, and the behaviors they demonstrate related to autism will be unique to them.

Table 11.3 Typical Interview Questions Rephrased for Autistic Candidates

Question Type	Typically Phrased	Rephrased
Behavioral	Tell me about a time you were the new member on a team. How did you earn their trust?	Tell me about a time you were asked to join a school or work project team that had already been working together. What did you do to introduce yourself to your schoolmates/ colleagues on the team and let them know what you could do to contribute to the team's goals?
Opinion	How would your boss from your last job describe you?	Based on feedback you received, what do you think your boss at your last job would say are your strengths and areas where you could use further development if I were to ask him/her?
Brain-teaser	How much would you charge to wash every window in NYC?	If you owned a window washing company and a client asked you for a bid to wash every window in NYC, but you physically couldn't count all the windows, describe to me the process you would go through to estimate the number of windows in NYC so that you could determine a price for your client?

Artificial Intelligence

In acknowledgment of the limitations of intuitive hiring practices, we are starting to see the development and adoption of new technologies to further a more scientific approach to recruiting. The advent of artificial intelligence and big data is allowing technology to transform the recruiting world with on-demand video interviewing and assessment platforms. These platforms – over a dozen are available on the market now[17] – are designed to, among other things, remove some of the inherent biases from the interview process. Rather than rely on an interviewer's instincts or intuition about candidates, most on-demand video interviewing platforms utilize machine learning, natural language processing, and some level of facial motion processing to determine the relevance of a candidate's answers and their use of language. The questions asked and reliance on certain features of the platforms, such as facial motion processing, can be adjusted for the jobs being considered, e.g. those requiring significant customer interactions versus those that do not. While questions exist about whether these platforms eliminate *all* forms of bias, or actually create other types of bias, it is important to understand their advantages and disadvantages when considering autistic candidates.

Analytics have been used to increase effectiveness in recruiting for some time. In 2006, Google implemented a hiring system called the Rule of Four.[18] The premise was simple. After exhaustive study, Google found that four interviews were sufficient to choose a successful candidate, and that additional interviews often yielded diminishing returns.

They also found that the aggregated ratings of four interviewers resulted in better hiring decisions than the ratings of any single interviewer. Another benefit for Google was that the applicant experience improved when they limited the number of interviews to no more than four.

So what is needed to implement a system like the Rule of Four? In order to aggregate the results of multiple interviewers, a *structured interview* approach is needed. Each interviewer should have pre-assigned questions to cover that allow the candidate's answers to be consistently measured and aggregated. Interviewers cannot treat interviews as a free form discussion with candidates, with the goal of "getting to know" them. Irrelevant questions, such as "What is your favorite color?" or "What are your hobbies?" should not be asked, as these provide no information about a candidate's ability to do the job and the answers cannot be measured. For neurodivergent candidates, providing this structure removes some of the typical interview challenges, eliminates questions irrelevant in determining a candidate's skills for the job, and neutralizes the impact of one bad interview.

For those organizations that have or are implementing an online video interviewing platform, considering how to best serve neurodivergent candidates is key to ensuring your platform and processes are not inadvertently biased against this population. To start, most video interviewing platforms allow employers to screen candidate resumes, conduct asynchronous (one-way) or live interviews, and perform skills assessments. Ideally, the platform chosen is programmed for unbiased resume parsing and unstructured data scoring, meaning the algorithms are written to score the meaning of what the candidate is saying or writing, not necessarily how they say it and if they are looking at the camera while they talk.

Assessment features that are skills-based can be particularly useful, as they can provide candidates with the opportunity to try out the job. But most importantly, previewing the process with autistic candidates (as discussed in Chapter 5) will provide them with the information they need to minimize their anxiety by allowing them to prepare for successfully completing video interviews. To view sample handouts for both employers and autistic jobseekers developed by HireVue and Integrate Autism Employment Advisors for users of HireVue's video interviewing platform, go to: www.integrateadvisors.org/hirevue-tips-sheet.

Conclusion

Typical interviews employ "what-if" scenarios and opinion/behavioral questions as predictors of job success, as many interviewers are looking to determine a candidate's *mindset* as much as they are their *skill set*. For autistic jobseekers, who can have difficulty understanding the perspective of others and can be literal, deliberative thinkers, this approach creates disadvantages for them during the interview process. Interviewers who are aware of this should phrase questions in a clear and direct manner, creating a more successful interview experience for neurodivergent candidates. Additionally, the emerging use of on-demand video interviewing platforms that employ artificial intelligence can remove bias from the hiring process and provide a structured and more comfortable interview process for neurodivergent candidates.

Notes

1 Merriam-Webster Dictionary. s.v. "Mindset." February 8, 2021. https://www.merriam-webster.com/dictionary/mindset.
2 Dweck, Carol S. *Mindset: The New Psychology of Success*. New York: Ballantine Books, 2016.
3 Tower, Jessica. "How to Hire for Growth Mindset with One Interview Question." March 27, 2017. http://jesstower.com/how-to-hire-for-growth-mindset-with-one-interview-question/.
4 Dweck, Carol S. "What Having a 'Growth Mindset' Actually Means." *Harvard Business Review*, January 13, 2016. https://hbr.org/2016/01/what-having-a-growth-mindset-actually-means.
5 Boss, Jeff. "5 Questions That Identify Growth-Minded Employees." *Entrepreneur*, May 22, 2015. https://www.entrepreneur.com/article/246494.
6 Cohen, Liz. "5 Reasons Growth Mindset Candidates Get the Job." *Next Step Careers*, March 10, 2021. http://ns-careers.com/blog/growthmindset.
7 Kahneman, Daniel. *Thinking, Fast and Slow*. New York: Farrar, Straus and Giroux, 2013.
8 Scheiner, Marcia, and Joan Bogden. *An Employer's Guide to Managing Professionals on the Autism Spectrum*. London: Jessica Kingsley, 2017.
9 Morsanyi, Kinga, and Ruth M. J. Byrne, eds. *Thinking, Reasoning, and Decision Making in Autism*. London: Routledge, 2020.
10 Lebowitz, Shana, Allana Akhtar, and Marguerite Ward. "61 Cognitive Biases That Screw Up Everything We Do." *Business Insider*, May 5, 2020. https://www.businessinsider.com/cognitive-biases-2015-10.
11 Tulshyan, Ruchika. "How to Reduce Personal Bias When Hiring." *Harvard Business Review*, June 28, 2019. https://hbr.org/2019/06/how-to-reduce-personal-bias-when-hiring.
12 Haden, Jeff. "Why the Wrong Candidate Sometimes Gets Hired: Harvard Research Reveals People Prefer 'Naturals' Even When They Claim to Value Hard Work a Lot More." *Inc.*, May 19, 2020. https://www.inc.com/jeff-haden/why-wrong-candidate-sometimes-gets-hired-harvard-research-reveals-people-prefer-naturals-even-when-they-claim-to-value-hard-work-a-lot-more.html.
13 World Economic Forum. "Want to Achieve Success? Develop a Strategic Mindset." July 6, 2020. https://www.weforum.org/agenda/2020/07/strategic-mindset-success/.
14 Grant, Stephanie, Frank Hodge, and Samantha Seto. "Can a Deliberative Mindset Prompt Reduce Investors' Reliance on Fake News?" *SSRN Electronic Journal*, February 19, 2021. https://ssrn.com/abstract=3444228.

15 Ashwin, Chris, and Mark Brosnan. "The Dual Process Theory of Autism." In Morsanyi, Kinga and Ruth M. J. Byrne, eds. *Thinking, Reasoning, and Decision Making in Autism*, 27–28. London: Routledge, 2020.
16 Carson, Biz. "Google's Infamous Brain-Teaser Interview Questions Don't Predict Performance." *Business Insider*, October 6, 2015. https://www.businessinsider.co m/google-brain-teaser-interview-questions-dont-work-2015-10.
17 Integrate Autism Employment Advisors entered into service agreements with HireVue, one such platform, in 2019 to provide advice on the use of their video interviewing platform for neurodiverse jobseekers and to recruit an intern and provide autism in the workplace training to HireVue staff.
18 Thompson, Derek. "The Science of Smart Hiring." *The Atlantic*, April 10, 2016. https://www.theatlantic.com/business/archive/2016/04/the-science-of-smart-h iring/477561/.

Part IV

The First 100 Days

Chapter 12

Getting the Candidate to "Yes"

In the recruiting world, a key metric is the offer acceptance rate (OAR). Simply calculated, as shown in Figure 12.1, the OAR is:[1]

$$\text{Offer Acceptance Rate} = \left(\frac{\text{Number of offers accepted}}{\text{Number of offers}} \right) \times 100$$

Figure 12.1 Offer Acceptance Rate Formula.

For employers, the higher one's OAR, the better. Ideally, every candidate offered a job would accept but, unfortunately, this is not the reality of the recruiting world. According to the website Glassdoor.com, the top three reasons candidates turn down job offers are: [2]

1. Better salary and benefits elsewhere
2. A poor candidate experience during the recruiting/interview process
3. Negative reputation of the employer

While it may seem counterintuitive that an autistic jobseeker, who has struggled with unemployment, would turn down a seemingly competitive job offer, it does happen. Not only will someone on the spectrum turn down an offer of employment for one of the reasons above, they may also not accept a job for one of the following reasons:

1. Lack of clarity around the role and responsibilities of the position
2. Concern about their ability to do the job
3. Uncertainty over the time commitment required
4. Anxiety about potential relocation

Regardless of the reason(s) for turning down your offer, it is costly to lose a candidate you want to hire.

When hiring autistic individuals, the process of "getting the candidate to yes" can require additional attention in the final stages of the offer process. This chapter discusses how to clearly communicate the many aspects of an offer of employment to the autistic candidate, including the terms of the offer, required drug testing, the process for reference checking, and relocation assistance, if necessary.

Making the Offer

As has been discussed throughout this book, most autistic jobseekers struggle to find work. While they may have interviewed with several different employers and have some familiarity with the interview process, they are less likely to have received any job offers. As a result, they are not experienced in the process of reviewing and accepting official offers of employment. Additionally, these candidates may be uncertain about taking on a new role in an unfamiliar environment and will experience increased levels of anxiety when faced with the decision of whether to accept or reject an offer.

Even after successfully completing an interview process and receiving an offer, some autistic individuals will question if they have the skill sets to do the job. Similar to the way these candidates self-select out of applying for jobs when reading position descriptions (as discussed in Chapter 7) or tend to focus on their weaknesses rather than their strengths during interviews (as discussed in Chapter 11), they may reject a job offer if they have any uncertainty about their ability to meet the demands of the role successfully or are unclear as to the actual job requirements. Therefore, it is critical that job offers be clear and complete.

Some employers extend a verbal offer prior to a written offer, looking for the candidate to indicate they will accept before finalizing all the terms in writing. While letting autistic individuals know an offer will be coming is fine, expecting an acceptance of the offer before providing all the terms in writing is discouraged. To properly review and process the job offer, having the complete information in writing is important for autistic candidates. This will allow them time to process the information, identify any questions they might have, and seek out a trusted advisor for guidance, thereby reducing the likelihood of rejection of the job offer due to misunderstandings between the oral and written offers.

At a minimum, the job offer should include the following in writing:

- Job title
- Job description
- Start date
- Reporting structure
- Work location, including any adjustments made as an accommodation
- Work hours, including any adjustments made as an accommodation
- A sample work schedule for an average workday, if possible

- Required travel, if any
- Required overtime, if any
- Compensation: salary and bonus, if any
- Available benefits
- Paid time off (holidays, vacation days, sick days)
- Pending requirements, if any
- Contact person for questions

When extending the offer, contact the candidate to let them know how it will be delivered (i.e., by email, regular mail, Fedex, or some other form), when to expect it, and ask them to confirm receipt with you. If they do not receive the offer by a certain date, instruct them how to notify you. Set a fixed date by which they must provide you with their formal decision on the offer, how to accept the offer, and a contact person for questions while the candidate is making their decision.

Remember that autistic individuals can be deliberative thinkers, as discussed in Chapter 11, so be sure to give the candidate enough time to decide. Candidates who are deliberative thinkers and feel rushed may be reluctant to ask for more time to consider the terms and, consequently, turn down the offer because of uncertainty or anxiety. If the candidate seems uncertain, offer to have them come in for another tour of the offices and an informal conversation with the hiring manager or key colleagues. Also, if the candidate needs to pass a drug test or reference screening before the offer is considered final, be sure to clearly state that, or any other requirements, in the offer letter.

Drug Testing

Pre-employment drug testing is a common condition of job offers. For autistic candidates, however, the drug test can present another hurdle in the employment process. Two areas of potential concern exist for autistic individuals when faced with the prospect of taking a drug test.

First, some individuals on the spectrum take medications related to autism that are prescribed and managed by medical professionals and are necessary for the individual's well-being. Some of these medications may be detected through drug testing, requiring autistic individuals to disclose sensitive medical information they would rather not share. In order to allow autistic candidates with medication concerns to meet drug testing requirements, employers need to provide avenues for disclosure that address the strict privacy concerns of their autistic employees.

Second, a few individuals on the spectrum may experience extreme performance anxiety when having to complete a drug test within a tight timeframe. This anxiety can result in the individual being unable to deliver the required specimen for the test at the time needed. As emphasized throughout this book, the goal of your entire interviewing and recruiting process should be to minimize candidates' anxiety, and the approach to drug testing should be no different. Provide candidates with ample notice that drug testing will be required if an offer is extended. Let them know in advance of an offer how long they will have from the offer date to complete the drug test and who they should communicate with if they have any concerns about this portion of their onboarding process. This will allow the candidates who may experience anxiety around drug testing to plan in advance and reduce their anxiety. Waiving the drug testing requirement should be considered an accommodation for those candidates who provide a valid request.

Reference Checking

Reference checking can be a useful tool in predicting a candidate's performance on the job. We all know, however, that most individuals provide references with whom they have a good relationship and who will give a strong recommendation. For autistic individuals, given their social communication struggles, they may not have access to the same number or level of references as their neurotypical peers. Not only have many of them not built strong relationships with prior managers/colleagues or professors, but they may have had situations where they were undisclosed and the environment was not autism friendly, resulting in a poor work experience. In some cases, they may have no work experience at all. This may leave them unable to provide the standard professional references from prior employers or professors.

When requesting references from autistic candidates, encourage them to identify individuals who can provide insights into their work-related strengths and weaknesses. If you have a set list of questions you ask the references, provide it to the candidate so they can think about whom they know who will be able to answer those questions about them. If a candidate struggles to provide professional references, be flexible in allowing them to identify individuals who will be able to opine on their skill sets related to the position. You might suggest to the candidate, "I am willing to accept a reference from someone who you know well and can tell me about your skill sets and ability to do this job". These references may be academic counselors who supported the candidate in school, staff members who worked with the candidate at autism support programs, or sourcing partners discussed in Chapter 8. Other sources of reference may be the leader of a support group the candidate attends or the coach or mentor of an extracurricular activity in which the candidate participates.

You may find that some types of references you receive from autistic candidates are not what you are used to, such as the leader of an Eagle Scout group or a vocational services job coach. Just as you need to review resumes of applicants on the spectrum differently than you might that of a neurotypical candidate (as discussed in Chapter 6), so should you consider non-standard references for autistic individuals, as these might be the people in the best position to tell you about the candidate. Remember, however, it is up to the candidate to offer these references: only discuss a candidate's autism with a reference if the candidate has provided permission for you to do so.

Relocation Assistance

Relocating for work is common in the US. In a 2019 survey conducted by Robert Half, a global staffing firm, 62% of workers said they would consider moving for a job. This percentage is even higher among 18 to 34-year-olds at 76%.[3] Over half of young adults in their 20s live independently and are mobile. Yet only one in five autistic young adults live independently.[4] This makes relocating for a job that much more difficult.

Autistic individuals can be dependent on family members for assistance with activities such as food shopping, cooking, cleaning, laundry, and managing finances. For those who struggle socially, their family members may also be their main source of social interaction and an important factor in staving off loneliness. In addition to the support of family members, an autistic candidate may rely on a network of clinical or therapeutic support providers, including a psychologist, psychiatrist, speech and language therapist, life skills coach, and support group. The importance of this carefully constructed support environment should not be underestimated in how it will impact a candidate's success on the job. That is not to say that some autistic individuals cannot and will not move for the right position. Many autistic individuals have successfully lived away from home while attending college and are open to moving for the right career opportunity. Relocation, however, needs to be approached with forethought and planning.

If relocation is going to be required for a position, or may be required in the future, candidates should be informed upfront. Some candidates will decline to pursue roles requiring relocation, so it is best to know this beforehand. For those willing to move, employers should consider providing the following as part of relocation assistance:

- *Temporary housing* until the candidate can decide on and secure a permanent home. Remember that some autistic individuals are deliberative thinkers and the process of finding a new home may take them more time in order to minimize stress and anxiety.
- *Home search services* focusing on identifying appropriate neighborhoods if candidates need to be within walking distance of public transportation and daily living services for those who do not drive.
- An *employee assistance program* to identify appropriate medical, clinical, and/or therapeutic professionals the candidate may need to engage in their new location.
- A *mentor* to serve as a guide to the new location. Someone, preferably a peer from the company, to act as a social guide to introduce the

candidate to the local services – shopping, entertainment venues, parks and recreation, restaurants, etc.

For jobs that require extensive travel, similar concerns can arise. Not all autistic candidates will be comfortable spending a significant amount of time adapting to new environments, be it different hotels, restaurants, or time zones, on a regular basis. When it comes to relocation and travel, however, these issues can be as true for neurotypical candidates as they are for neuro-divergent ones.

> Not all autistic individuals will present the same. No two individuals on the spectrum are affected by autism the same way, and the behaviors they demonstrate related to autism will be unique to them.

Conclusion

Being thoughtful in the process of extending job offers to autistic jobseekers is critical to the acceptance of the offer. Make sure the terms of an offer are clearly and comprehensively spelled out in writing. Preview your requirements around reference checking and drug testing with candidates, working with them to offer any necessary accommodations. For candidates who are relocating, provide assistance that will allow them to settle into their new environment with the necessary supports. These strategies will help avoid misunderstandings, reduce stress and anxiety for candidates, and facilitate mutual success as they start their new jobs.

Notes

1 Biko, Nikoletta. "Job Offer Acceptance Rate Metrics: Recruiting Metrics FAQ." *Workable*, September 15, 2017. https://resources.workable.com/tutorial/faq-job -offer-metrics (Figure 12.1).
2 Moore, Emily. "The Most Common Reasons Candidates Reject Job Offers (& How You Can Prevent It!)." *Glassdoor for Employers*, July 26, 2018. https://ww w.glassdoor.com/employers/blog/common-reasons-reject-job-offers/.
3 Robert Half. "62 Percent of Workers Would Relocate for a Job, Survey Finds." *Robert Half*, January 1, 2015. http://rh-us.mediaroom.com/2019-01-15-62-Perc ent-Of-Workers-Would-Relocate-For-A-Job-Survey-Finds.
4 Roux, Anne M., Paul T. Shattuck, Jessica E. Rast, Julianna A. Rava, and Kristy A. Anderson. *National Autism Indicators Report: Transition into Young Adulthood.* Philadelphia, PA: Life Course Outcomes Research Program, A.J. Drexel Autism Institute, Drexel University, 2015.

Chapter 13

Onboarding New Hires

Congratulations! You've hired a new employee and they are starting with your organization. You are excited. The new hire is excited too, but there is also a good chance they are anxious as well. Major changes in our lives – a new job, a move, getting married – can all be happy events, yet they all cause anxiety. For autistic individuals, who may already live with heightened levels of anxiety (see Chapter 4), beginning a new job can be particularly difficult.

First-day jitters are normal for anyone approaching a new situation with unfamiliar people, but for individuals who struggle with social cognitive challenges, the time needed to feel comfortable in their new workplace may take longer than is typical. As a result, it is important to have well-thought-out orientation and onboarding practices in place. In this chapter, we will discuss how to ensure your orientation and onboarding practices provide the support critical to the success of autistic hires.

Onboarding vs. Orientation

The first step in creating successful orientation and onboarding practices is understanding that they are not the same thing. *Orientation* is a one-time event, and may include:

- *Introducing* new employees to your organization's mission, vision, and values
- *Familiarizing* new employees with general information about your organization's activities
- *Presenting* benefit plans information
- *Explaining* company rules
- *Touring* the physical space

Most orientation sessions last anywhere from a couple of hours to a full day. Depending on the size of the employer, they may be delivered on an as-needed basis for a new employee or on pre-scheduled dates for large groups of new hires.

Onboarding is an ongoing process that occurs over the course of an employee's first months, or even up to a year, on the job. During this time, the new hire develops a deeper understanding of the function of their department in the organization, their role within the department, how to perform their tasks, and how to navigate the organization to best perform in their role. Data shows that onboarding programs can increase retention by 25% and that employees who participate in a structured onboarding program are 69% more likely to remain with their employer after three years.[1]

When autistic individuals obtain their first professional position, most will never have experienced a proper orientation and/or onboarding. Therefore, they may not know what to expect or ask for when joining a new organization and can be hesitant to speak up if they don't receive the information they need. Even those who have gone through this process with other employers will need a well-structured orientation and onboarding process, as the move to the new workplace can be a dramatic change. Autistic candidates may not transfer the learning from those prior experiences, as some people on the spectrum are more likely to notice differences rather than similarities when dealing with previous processes or situations (see Chapter 5 for a discussion of generalization).

Orientation

After the offer, orientation is typically the second welcome a new employee receives from their employer. The candidates have spent a lot of effort trying to make a good impression on you to get the offer, and now it is your opportunity to create a good impression on your new hire. This is no different for autistic employees than it is for any employee. For autistic individuals, however, the orientation process should start earlier than the first day and include additional steps to reduce candidates' anxiety and provide additional support in the administrative aspects of becoming an official employee.

Pre-Orientation

When I started my first job out of college for a global financial services organization, orientation was a one-day event held in a central auditorium for well over 100 employees who had started in the past month. The day consisted of several videos, presentations by senior executives and human resource staff, the distribution of binders with company policies and forms to be completed, and a one-hour, unstructured lunch break. The attendees were from all areas of the organization and had started anywhere from one to 30 days from the date of the orientation session. It was a day filled with an overwhelming amount of information and required follow-up in terms of completing and returning new employee forms. It was also a day that could provide challenges for anyone who is overwhelmed by large crowds of strangers, an excess of information, and/or environments with harsh lighting or loud noises. Any of these challenges could make an orientation like this counter-productive for a newly-hired autistic employee.

Subjecting new hires who are on the spectrum to an orientation event that may be difficult for them to navigate can be avoided by holding what we call a *pre-orientation*, a briefing for candidates by their human resources representative a week before their start date. This meeting can serve several purposes:

- First, preview with the candidates what will occur during the formal orientation session (see Chapter 5 for more on *previewing*). During this discussion, you can provide a schedule of the upcoming orientation (see Table 13.1 for a sample schedule) and discuss any challenges and appropriate accommodations (see below for more information on suggested accommodations).

Table 13.1 Sample Orientation Schedule

Time	Activity	Partner(s)	Location
9:00 – 9:15 a.m.	Check-in	-	Main Auditorium
9:15 – 10:15 a.m.	Senior management welcome and presentations	-	Main Auditorium
10:15 – 10:30 a.m.	Break	-	
10:30 – 11:30 a.m.	Overview of benefits	-	Main Auditorium
11:30 a.m. – noon	Signing of benefits and new employee forms	-	Main Auditorium
Noon – 1:00 p.m.	Lunch	J.Smith/M. Brown	Employee Café
1:00 – 2:00 p.m.	Review of company values and policies	-	Main Auditorium
2:00 – 2:30 p.m.	Photo/badge/security setup	L.Green	Security Office, Building 401, Lobby level
2:30 – 2:45 p.m.	Break	-	
2:45 – 3:30 p.m.	Technology setup – computer/phone pickup	L.Green	Technology Suite, Building 401, 3rd fl
3:30 – 5:00 p.m.	Join team – workstation setup and meet teammates	J.Smith	Building 301, 2nd fl

- Second, if the candidates were hired as part of an Autism@Work initiative, and more than one employee from the program is starting at that time, use this session to bring together the new autistic employees to meet each other. This will allow the new hires to recognize some familiar faces when they attend the orientation, as well as on their first day of work.

- Third, show the candidates their new workstation (assuming an in-office situation) and allow them to bring some personal items to set up at their desks.
- Fourth, provide any paperwork that needs to be completed at the orientation so the candidates can review it at home beforehand, allowing them to consult with others on selecting certain benefit plans if they need to do so.
- Fifth, if you can, have certain executives or key staff who are presenting at the orientation meet with the new hires briefly when they come in for a short introduction, allowing the candidates to feel more at ease at the actual session.

Orientation Accommodations

As in my own orientation experience described earlier, not all orientation sessions occur on an employee's first day. If this is a practice in your organization, it is recommended that you schedule the start date of autistic hires to coincide with an orientation date. This can help smooth their transition into the organization by providing context about the broader organization, its rules and policies, as well as handle the administrative aspects of becoming an employee in a structured format. Having orientation on day one helps reduce the uncertainty that many new employees feel, thereby easing feelings of anxiety.

If your orientation process is a large group session, consider assigning a partner or "buddy" to attend some or all the sessions with the new hire. For candidates who find it particularly difficult to engage in group activities, offer to have someone they have met during their pre-orientation session meet them at the beginning of the day to join them throughout the day. For individuals who are comfortable attending on their own for large group presentations, have teammates they've already met and/or the hiring manager meet them at a prearranged time and place to take them to lunch and accompany them to setup activities.

Part of any orientation process is the completion of forms for compliance purposes, payroll, and benefits. As discussed above, it is best to provide these forms to autistic individuals beforehand. If you do so, make sure the forms are accompanied by clear instructions about when the completed information needs to be returned. If you cannot provide these forms prior to a new hire's first day, allow them time to take the forms home to review and complete. If you need the forms completed and returned on the day of the orientation, provide a contact person in your organization who will be available to answer any questions regarding the completion of the forms. Even if the new hire can take the forms home, make sure they have contact information for someone who can answer any questions they may have when completing the forms.

It is not uncommon on orientation day, despite everyone's best efforts, for some new hires to experience problems receiving their employee badge and proper technology setup. Again, because of lack of experience with these types of issues, this can be particularly upsetting for autistic candidates who may become overly anxious with deviations in the expected time frame for these activities. As can be seen previously in Table 13.1, we recommend having a buddy or partner go with a new hire on the spectrum for these tasks as well. If a problem occurs, the partner or buddy should be able to explain what the process is to rectify the situation, how long it should take, and what will happen in the interim to ensure the employee can get started in their new role. Additionally, if you are embarking on a broader neurodiversity and/or autism hiring initiative, inform your security and technology teams that this effort is underway in the organization. You should also provide these teams with training to ensure they are communicating effectively and respectfully with their autistic colleague (see the section in Chapter 14 on awareness training).

Finally, for those autistic individuals who may find a day like the one shown in Table 13.1 to be overwhelming, consider excusing them from your formal orientation process. Instead, ensure the individual receives the information in small or one-on-one sessions spread out over a few days either before they start or within their first couple of weeks. Remember, part of the purpose of the orientation process is to make sure the employee has a basic level of information about your organization and to start them off with a great impression of the place they have chosen to work. For autistic individuals, showing them the flexibility they may need for that process to occur goes a long way to achieving those things.

Onboarding

Onboarding, also referred to as *organizational socialization*, is the process through which new hires go from being outsiders to becoming insiders of your organization. During this time, employees not only gain knowledge and skills, they learn the behaviors that will make them successful on the job. Talya Bauer, Professor of Management at Portland State University, has developed a model for successful onboarding that incorporates what she's coined the "Four Cs":[2]

- <u>Compliance:</u> teaching employees basic legal and policy-related rules and regulations
- <u>Clarification:</u> ensuring that employees understand their new jobs and all related expectations
- <u>Culture:</u> providing employees with a sense of organizational norms – both formal and informal
- <u>Connection:</u> creating vital interpersonal relationships and information networks

Almost all employers cover the first "C", compliance, in their orientation session. Unfortunately, some employers never make it past this step, leaving new hires to observe and understand the cultural norms and develop their own informal and formal networks on their own. For autistic employees to be successful (and really for all employees to be successful), it is important to include all four of these Cs in your onboarding process.

The entire burden of completing a successful onboarding process should not be the sole responsibility of the managers of autistic employees. Multiple resources can be drawn upon, internally and externally, to create a supportive onboarding program. These can include training programs, job coaches, buddies, and mentors. If autistic peer buddies/mentors are available within your organization, include them as part of the onboarding support network for new hires. It is important to remember that autistic employees, particularly those who struggle to understand hidden curriculum issues, should not be expected to take the lead in guiding their own onboarding process.

Make It Clear

From day one, it is critical that autistic individuals understand what their role is on the job. In Chapter 7 we discussed the importance of clear job descriptions in attracting autistic applicants. It is equally important that a new hire on the spectrum have a clear description of their role and responsibilities. Many autistic individuals like structure and want to know what is expected of them. If thrust into a job where new tasks and responsibilities are constantly arising, an autistic employee may become overly anxious and agitated.[3] By providing detailed project plans with tasks, assignments, deadlines, and interdependencies clearly defined, the chance for misunderstandings should be minimized.

Many new employees engage in training when starting a new job. These training courses may be to learn a new system, a new process, or company procedures/rules. To the extent you will have training requirements for your autistic hires, provide a schedule of the sessions upfront. Discuss the purpose behind each training session and how it relates to the employee's tasks or role in the organization. Let them know the expected timing to complete the training sessions and how long each one should take. If your organization has a learning platform that is available to employees to take training courses at will, discuss what is appropriate for the individual and how to balance any desire to do additional training against the required workload.

Decode Your Unwritten Rules

Every organization has a unique culture, and seasoned professionals know that working for one company can feel completely different than working for another company, or even within different departments or divisions of the same company. Many autistic individuals struggle to understand the unwritten rules in the workplace that define an organization's culture (see the discussion of hidden curriculum in Chapter 4). Consequently, most individuals on the spectrum who lose their jobs are fired for social missteps at work – often without having a clear understanding as to why.

Providing clear and consistent direction to autistic employees about the unwritten rules of your work environment is critical to their success. Although each event in isolation may seem minor, small missteps compounded over time can become a significant problem. Examples of hidden curriculum issues that should be addressed clearly during an onboarding period may include:

- Who to copy on emails
- When to take lunch
- What to wear to certain company meetings/events
- What it means when a senior executive says "I have an open-door policy"
- How long to talk when giving an update in staff meetings
- What is an appropriate topic of conversation at the lunch room table
- How long to wait before pinging your boss if they haven't responded to an instant message
- Who to contact with technology problems

Direction on the unwritten rules of your work environment should come from the individual's direct supervisor, HR support, or a close colleague. When addressing situations that require clarification of hidden curriculum issues, always talk to the individual in a one-on-one setting, not in front of others. The goal is to coach the new employee with respectful feedback, explaining the norms of your organization's culture and how they could have handled the situation or interaction more effectively. For certain situations, if a hard-and-fast rule exists, provide it. For example, if an employee struggles with who to copy on emails, the rule may be "always copy your supervisor and they will let you know if anyone else needs to be included on the email chain".

Provide a "Coach"

Being the "new kid on the block" is never easy, whether it's moving to a new town or starting a new job. Autistic individuals who struggle with social interactions and understanding the cultural norms of an organization will have a particularly hard time developing both the formal and informal relationships that most employees begin to form during an onboarding period. In order to assist autistic employees in successfully integrating into your organization, it is useful to have individuals who can serve as coaches.

Coaches for people with autism can come in a few forms. A *job coach*, in the formal meaning, for a person with a disability is a professional who has been trained to come into the workplace with the employee to support them in being successful on the job. This can range from teaching and supporting them with their assigned tasks, to helping them navigate the organizational rules, both written and unwritten. Job coaches are typically provided by a vocational services organization that serves the individual and are available for up to 90 days. Most professional hires with autism do not need a job coach to help them with their assigned tasks. Some, however, may benefit from having a job coach as they start their new positions to help them organize themselves, establish a routine, and provide feedback on interactions with key teammates.

A more common form of coaching for autistic professionals is achieved through mentors who can be both internal and external to your organization. It is not uncommon for autistic individuals to have *external mentors*, such as a therapist or life skills coach, whom they see on a regular basis. This person can be an ally in coaching the new employee on how to engage successfully with colleagues. Due to privacy issues, employers cannot encourage their autistic employees to seek outside coaching help or ask about what services they are receiving. As a sourcing partner working with employers, we have served as an intermediary between external coaches and employers for autistic candidates who asked us to do so.

Internal mentors can oftentimes be the most effective way of ensuring a smooth integration of autistic hires into your organization. Once a candidate has settled into their new role, after two to three months, assign a mentor from outside of the individual's group to serve as a mentor. The role of the mentor is to help the autistic employee continue to learn about broader organizational norms (i.e., career development and goal setting) and develop a network. A mentor–mentee relationship for autistic hires should be well-defined and highly structured. Prior to launching a mentor–mentee program, both the mentors and mentees should go through training. For the mentors, ensure they are familiar with autism and the challenges related to executive functioning and the hidden curriculum that their mentee may encounter in the workplace. For mentees, define the parameters of a mentor–mentee relationship and provide guidance on how to get the most out of the interactions. We recommend regularly scheduled meetings with a preset agenda. Example 13.1 in the Appendix lists mentor–mentee guidelines we use with Integrate clients.

Conclusion

In many respects, the real work in successfully hiring autistic individuals begins after they have accepted your job offer. The retention of new hires on the spectrum will be influenced by the effectiveness of your orientation and onboarding processes. While orientation is typically a one-time event, onboarding should continue until the employee is fully transitioned into their role and the broader organization. For some individuals, this can take weeks, for others many months. Done properly, orientation and onboarding will result in employees who understand their roles and responsibilities and are functioning well within the norms and culture of your organization.

Notes

1 Patankar, Vinay. "6 Checklists to Perfect Your New Employee Onboarding Process." *Process Street* (blog), February 2, 2018. https://www.process.st/new-employee-onboarding-process/.
2 Bauer, Talya N. "Onboarding New Employees: Maximizing Success." *SHRM Foundation*, 2010, 2. https://www.shrm.org/foundation/ourwork/initiatives/resources-from-past-initiatives/Documents/Onboarding%20New%20Employees.pdf.
3 For more information on managing these situations, see our companion book, *An Employer's Guide to Managing Professionals on the Autism Spectrum*, Chapter 11.

Chapter 14

Preparing Your Organization for Success

A high offer acceptance rate, as described in Chapter 12, is only a success if the candidates hired stay with your organization. Anyone who works in human resources or manages a business knows that it is costly to hire and train new employees. If employees join but do not stay with your organization, the resulting turnover can become a financial and morale drain on your business.

Similar to calculating an offer acceptance rate, as seen in Figure 14.1, you can determine your organization's *employee retention rate*[1] as follows:

$$\text{Employee Retention Rate} = \left(\frac{\text{Total \# of Employees} - \text{\# of Employees Who Left}}{\text{Total \# of Employees}} \right) \times 100$$

Figure 14.1 Employee Retention Rate Formula.

Calculating your retention rate is only useful, however, if you understand why employees leave and take corrective actions to retain talent. According to the Work Institute's *2020 Retention Report*, the top three reasons employees left a job in 2019 were:

- Career development – 20%
- Work–life balance – 12%
- Bad manager – 12%

The report goes on to state that 78% of the reasons given by employees for quitting are preventable by the employer.[2] In addition to the reasons cited for quitting in the Work Institute report, autistic employees may leave a job, or worse, get fired, due to:

- Bullying
- Sensory overload
- Social misunderstandings

Just as 78% of the reasons employees leave their jobs are preventable, so are these other reasons (listed above) that cause autistic individuals to leave their jobs.

Preparing your organization for integrating your new autistic hires is critical to strong retention. In this chapter, we will discuss how to prepare your organization for the newly hired autistic professional, including training and support of managers and colleagues, as well as easing the sensory and social demands of the workplace.

The Supportive Workplace

Organizations with well-established autism hiring programs, such as JPMorgan Chase, SAP, Microsoft, and EY, all report retention rates of over 90% among their autistic hires.[3] This high retention rate speaks not only to the desire of autistic individuals to remain in a role where they feel valued and have demonstrated success but includes the organizational preparation done by these employers to ensure a supportive workplace for employees on the spectrum, as these two go hand-in-hand.

Employers often assume that when an autistic individual enters the workforce they will need training and/or specialized support to "fit in" to their new work environment. They may expect the new employee to learn social skills that will allow them to interact effectively with colleagues and be successful at their jobs. It is equally important, however, that employers understand how to provide an environment that will allow autistic employees to feel comfortable bringing their whole selves to work.

Creating an environment that is conducive to the success of employees on the spectrum, as with any employee, allows them to perform at their best. While individuals on the spectrum can be prepared for what they will encounter when they go to work, they still bring with them a way of thinking and processing information, related to autism, that may translate into behavioral differences in the workplace.

Education and Training

Educating and training employees in your organization about autism and how to be supportive of autistic colleagues is an integral part of any successful autism hiring effort. Before starting, two points are important to understand.

First, *education and training are not the same thing*, and both need to be done. *Education* encompasses teaching employees in your organization about autism – the demographics of the autism population, how autism affects individuals, and how autistic colleagues may present in the workplace. *Training* is a more targeted effort in providing your employees with the skill sets to interact successfully and supportively with autistic co-workers. It is a false assumption that someone who knows about autism will intuitively know how to manage successfully or work cooperatively with someone on the spectrum.

Second, *general disability awareness education and training does not substitute for autism education and training.* This is not to say that disability awareness education and training isn't important. Approximately 20 million[4] Americans with a disability participate in the US labor force, and being a person with a disability is the only minority group that anyone can become a member of at any time in their life. However, general disability awareness training programs will not provide your employees with the depth of understanding and skill sets needed to work successfully with autistic colleagues. Typically, disability awareness training educates about various types of disabilities, with the goal of promoting empathy for individuals with disabilities and encouraging colleagues to look beyond an individual's disability and focus on their skill sets and talents. It does not teach managers and colleagues the specific strategies necessary to work with and support co-workers who may struggle with the specific challenges associated with autism or other disabilities.

Awareness Education

Creating a base of understanding of the talents and behavioral differences of autistic colleagues among your existing employees is the first step in preparing your organization. Given the incidence rate of autism, if you are a large employer (1,000 employees or more), chances are you already employ individuals on the autism spectrum. If you want to be an autism-friendly employer, broad-based autism awareness education in your organization is critical, regardless of whether or not you are actively seeking to hire additional autistic employees. Companies that have implemented neurodiversity and/or autism awareness education programs have also seen existing employees on the spectrum come forward and disclose an autism spectrum disorder diagnosis.

Autism awareness programs should, at a minimum, cover the following topics:

- Understanding neurodiversity – addressing the variations in cognitive thinking and processing
- Defining autism – what is the autism spectrum?
- Demographics
- Strengths of autistic talent
- Challenges/behavioral differences associated with autism and how they manifest in the workplace

In addition to the divisions/departments/units where an autism hiring effort is underway, offering this type of training to other areas of your organization can have a meaningful impact on the experience of autistic employees. Such departments might include security personnel and food services staff who may interact with autistic colleagues on a regular basis. Awareness training can be critical in helping staff in these departments understand interactions with which they may not be familiar. For example, should an autistic employee forget their ID badge and become anxious trying to enter the building or buying lunch, it will be helpful for the staff in these areas to have been educated about your autism hiring program. This will ensure they recognize that their autistic colleagues may need a more supportive and patient response than their neurotypical peers in anxiety-provoking situations.

This type of educational training can be delivered in multiple formats. Numerous organizations and individuals provide onsite, live training sessions or offer webinars covering these topics. Electronic training platforms are also available that offer short course format videos. If you are implementing an autism hiring program and working with a third-party organization to support you in that effort, they should be providing this training or helping you source the appropriate training support in this area. In the spirit of "nothing about us without us", if available, include autistic individuals in reviewing the training content and engage autistic volunteers in your organization to speak to colleagues about their experiences as an autistic jobseeker and worker.

Interviewing Training

In Part III we discussed how to create an autism-friendly interview process. Anyone involved in the interview process should have training that addresses how to conduct an effective interview process for autistic candidates. It is particularly helpful to have recruiters and hiring managers receive targeted training on what they might expect when meeting neurodivergent individuals. That training should, at a minimum, cover the following topics:

- How to evaluate the resume of autistic candidates
- Expectations around eye contact
- Engaging with candidates who provide too much or too little information
- Phrasing questions for maximum comprehension
- Recognizing and minimizing candidate anxiety
- Scheduling and previewing the interview process

As with autism awareness education, this type of training is available in multiple formats from different types of vendors. Additionally, some of the organizations that refer autistic candidates to your company (see Chapter 8) will be able to provide specific information to assist you in understanding how the candidates may present during the interview process. They may also be available to support both you and the candidate in the scheduling and follow-up process of the interview. If not, it will be even more important that your interviewers are knowledgeable about autism and how to conduct an interview process effectively with autistic jobseekers.

Management Training

Once candidates have accepted an offer, management training should be conducted for the direct supervisor, hiring manager, human resource business partner, and key colleagues of the new employee. This training should be tactical in nature, addressing day-to-day management situations that may arise. While this type of training cannot capture every scenario that may occur with a particular employee, the goal is to provide your team with the framework for learning an individual's working style, thinking through the challenge at hand, and developing clear communication skills.

The three main areas that should be covered in management training are the hidden curriculum, executive functioning, and sensory sensitivities (see Chapters 4 and 5 for further discussion of these topics). As mentioned above, not every situation that may occur when managing an autistic employee can be anticipated in a training session, but certain behaviors will appear more frequently with autistic colleagues than others. Suggested topics for management training are provided in Table 14.1.

Our companion book, *An Employer's Guide to Managing Professionals on the Autism Spectrum*, discusses how to address managing autistic professionals when faced with challenges in all these areas. Once again, if you are implementing an autism hiring program and working with a third-party

Table 14.1 Management Training Topics

Dealing with Hidden Curriculum Issues	• Literal thinking • Giving too much information • Non-verbal communication • Awkward social interactions • "Rude" behavior
Recognizing Executive Functioning Challenges	• Organization • Time management • Hyper-focus • Initiating • Prioritizing • Multi-tasking or transitioning • Working memory • Emotional regulation
Adjusting for Sensory Sensitivities	• Noise • Lighting • Smells • Touch • Repetitive behaviors or stimming

organization to support you in that effort, they should be providing this training or helping you source the appropriate training support in this area.

Autism awareness, interviewing, and management training will require some level of generalizing and stereotyping. Remember, no two individuals on the spectrum are affected by autism the same way, and the behaviors they demonstrate related to autism will be unique to them.

Manager Support

Much of the focus when starting an autism hiring effort is on the type of support that will be needed for the autistic employees being hired. However, the success of *any* employee is dependent not only on the new hire but their manager and their colleagues as well. Accordingly, it is important to focus on providing support for the employees who will be managing and working closely with your autistic talent. For individuals on the autism spectrum, being surrounded by a team of colleagues who know how to communicate effectively with them and can adapt to their working style is critically important. The preparatory training discussed above is only the first step in ensuring managers and co-workers are prepared to do this.

Ongoing access to experts and resources on managing autistic individuals will help your managers become better natural supports for your employees on the spectrum. If you are working with a third-party organization to implement your hiring initiative, find out what kind of support they provide to managers once candidates are on the job. At Integrate we recommend managers receive up to six months of transition support, starting with weekly check-in calls. If issues are occurring, you want to identify them and address them early. If you have multiple managers of autistic employees, hold group check-ins so that managers can share and learn from each other's experiences. This will also provide an early indication if a manager is not well suited for managing autistic individuals, allowing for a prompt course correction before the situation becomes untenable.

Office Environment

As discussed in Chapter 4, many autistic individuals struggle with sensory sensitivities that can be distracting and increase their level of anxiety. The office environment can be full of noises, smells, and visual stimuli that trigger these sensitivities in employees on the spectrum. Addressing these issues is not difficult if you are aware of the individual's needs. Therefore, it is important to ask your autistic employees if they have any sensory sensitivities.

Table 14.2 Accommodations for Sensory Sensitivities

Sound	• Allow to wear noise canceling headphones or earbuds
	• Seat away from noisy areas like hallways, restrooms, copy rooms, pantries, cafeterias, gathering areas, conference rooms, and entries/exits
	• Remove fluorescent light bulbs to eliminate humming/buzzing sounds
Visual Stimuli	• Allow to wear a hat with a brim to block out certain lights
	• Remove fluorescent light bulbs from over the employee's workspace
	• Use incandescent bulb desk lamps
	• Minimize visual field by avoiding seats that face busy areas
Smell	• Seat away from pantries, kitchenettes, and cafeterias
	• Use odor-free cleaning products
	• Have a fragrance-free workplace policy

Table 14.2 provides easy accommodations to ease the stress of sensory sensitivities for autistic colleagues.

Not everyone works in a formal office space. Many companies have moved away from the concept of an assigned desk and others have transitioned to working remotely full-time. If you are having your autistic employees come into the office, it is best to provide them with a dedicated space they use every time they are in the office. This will alleviate anxiety over having to find a space each time they are in the office and reduce the chances of the space not being ideal from a sensory perspective.

If your employees are working remotely, ensure they have a home setup that is consistent and distraction free. Suggest, if possible, individuals have a private space to work where they will not be disturbed by other members of their household. Establish a set schedule for each day that includes start time, breaks, lunchtime, and finish time, avoiding the scheduling of last-minute meetings. Additionally, ensure that colleagues on video conference calls have home office setups and virtual backgrounds that are distraction free. It can be difficult for anyone to concentrate if your colleague's cat is licking his face or ocean waves are crashing in the background.

Social Distractions and Demands

The 21st-century office can sometimes look more like an amusement park than a workplace. Activities ranging from ping pong to video games, go-carts, Olympic-size swimming pools, and professional gyms are available alongside dry cleaners, hair salons, indoor and outdoor cafes, and themed restaurants. In addition, some companies offer a multitude of training courses through their own "university" platforms, guest speakers, employee (or business) resource groups, and a variety of sports and activity teams. Providing these opportunities for relaxation and enrichment comes with the expectation that they will enhance, rather than negatively impact, work performance. The distractions of this type of work environment can be challenging for an autistic employee who struggles with time management or does not understand the unwritten rules about when and how to access all these amenities. If your organization offers extra amenities, such as these, be sure to provide clear guidelines in your onboarding materials about how and when employees are expected to use them.

Many organizations engage in social activities which, though "voluntary", are viewed as mandatory by most employees. These may include the annual holiday party and summer outing, monthly team gatherings, or colleague birthday parties. Some autistic individuals will look forward to these events and the opportunity to socialize with colleagues, while others will prefer to skip these gatherings. Regardless of the individual's preference, think through the social events your organization has beforehand, how they are structured, and the impact they may have on your autistic colleagues (i.e., are they held in crowded, noisy environments?). Decide which events are mandatory and which are not and make that clear to *all* employees. Provide your autistic colleagues an overview of the social schedule for the year, to the extent possible, and offer them a buddy, if they want, for the events they choose to attend. If they choose not to attend events that occur during working hours, let them know if they are required to be working during that time.

Conclusion

Preparing your organization to employ autistic individuals will result in a strong retention rate. According to a recent article in Forbes, the "true autism-friendly workplace" will go beyond physical accommodations of lighting and sound, and "be one with a culture that balances business needs with forms of greater patience and flexibility".[5] To that end, the goal of education and training and ongoing coaching for human resource professionals, managers, and colleagues should be creating effective natural supports for autistic employees in your organization. Understanding how to create an environment that is autism friendly by considering the appropriate office environment and social demands will lay the groundwork for autistic hires to succeed.

Notes

1 Workable. "What Is Employee Retention?" *Workable*, August 29, 2019. https://resources.workable.com/hr-terms/what-is-employee-retention (Figure 14.1).
2 Mahan, Thomas F., Danny Nelms, Jeeun Yi, Alexander T. Jackson, Michael Hein, and Richard Moffett. "2020 Retention Report: Trends, Reasons & Wake Up Call." *Work Institute*, 2020, 13. https://workinstitute.com/retention-report/.

3 Scheiner, Marcia. "The Autistic Workforce Is Here. Are You Prepared?" *Training Industry* (blog), March 16, 2020. https://trainingindustry.com/articles/strategy-alignment-and-planning/the-autistic-workforce-is-here-are-you-prepared/.
4 Division of Labor Force Statistics. "Persons with a Disability, 2019. Current Population Survey (CPS)." *US Bureau of Labor Statistics*, February 26, 2020. https://www.dol.gov/sites/dolgov/files/odep/pdf/dol-odep-2019-briefing-appended-submission.pdf.
5 Bernick, Michael. "The State of Autism Employment in 2021." *Forbes*, January 12, 2021. https://www.forbes.com/sites/michaelbernick/2021/01/12/the-state-of-autism-employment-in-2021/.

Chapter 15

Performance Issues

Successfully navigating the interview process and receiving an offer is just the start for autistic individuals. Another hurdle comes once the new hire is in their job and must prove themselves to their manager and colleagues. For the autistic employee, issues related to autism can often become obstacles once employed. People with autism may struggle to adjust to their new work environment due to challenges with the hidden curriculum, executive functioning, and anxiety. Without the appropriate understanding of these challenges, managers often decide employees on the spectrum are a poor cultural fit or lack the skill sets to do the job and terminate them.

The education and training discussed in Chapter 14 are critical in ensuring managers do not mistake these challenges as character or performance issues. In this chapter, we will introduce how hidden curriculum, executive functioning, and anxiety can have an impact on work performance and discuss mitigation strategies to facilitate employee success. For a more in-depth discussion of these issues and the management strategies for supporting autistic talent, see our book *An Employer's Guide to Managing Professionals on the Autism Spectrum*.

> Not all autistic individuals will present the same. No two individuals on the spectrum are affected by autism the same way, and the behaviors they demonstrate related to autism will be unique to them.

The Role of the Hidden Curriculum

As discussed in Chapter 4, the hidden curriculum is the unwritten rules that allow you to fit into any social situation. In the workplace, these rules can include, among other things, who to copy on emails, what to wear to work, what time to arrive at and leave the office, what to discuss at the lunch table, and how long to talk in meetings. Not only does every organization have its own hidden curriculum, the social rules of engagement within an organization may vary depending on when, where, and with whom you are interacting. Figuring out the hidden curriculum on a new job is a complex task for the most adept social thinkers. For autistic individuals, making social missteps at work can be quite common and is believed to be the number one cause of termination.

Most people can recall at least one colleague who never seemed to "fit in" or always said the wrong thing at the wrong time. Chances are this person was struggling to understand the hidden curriculum of their workplace. In our line of work, we constantly hear stories of individuals who are successful performers yet are terminated due to social mistakes. John* is a perfect example. Diagnosed with autism as an adult, John worked successfully as a chemical engineer for ten years without disclosing. Traditionally a loner, he was coached to engage more with his co-workers. John noticed his team always went to lunch together, so he began to join them. At lunch, John observed that his colleagues would discuss their hobbies. After a few weeks, John decided to start sharing his special interest at lunchtime. Unfortunately, John's hobby was researching torture techniques used by third-world dictators. As time went on, John would go into greater detail about his research, offending several of his colleagues. Rather than ask him to talk about something else, complaints were filed against John, and he was ultimately terminated for workplace harassment.

John was able to observe the obvious actions of his colleagues at lunchtime, such as eating together and talking about their hobbies. He could not, however, understand the more subtle social rules of what would be an appropriate hobby to discuss or interpret the negative reactions of his teammates, such as eye-rolling or a look of disgust, when he went into detail on inappropriate topics. Regardless of John's lack of disclosure, this situation could easily have been remedied if John's manager or HR business partner had taken him aside and explained that his special interest was not an appropriate topic for discussion in the workplace.

Employees with autism can learn to incorporate your organization's expectations of appropriate behavior with the proper coaching. Take the example of Sam, a recent college graduate Integrate placed as an intern in the human resources department of a global engineering firm. Given his new role, Sam took it upon himself to start reading all the articles he could find on human capital management in *Harvard Business Review*. After reading an article, Sam, who has a photographic memory, would come into the office and go to each of his colleagues and spend 20 minutes recounting for them what he'd learned from his reading. While his supervisor was pleased by his initiative, he also saw that Sam was taking up too much time from his colleagues and not understanding their non-verbal cues when they would look at their watches or turn back to their computers and start typing.

After discussing the situation with us, Sam's boss met with him and first praised him for taking the initiative to learn more about human capital management, then second, explained that he was taking too much of his colleague's working time sharing what he'd learned, and third, agreed on a time limit (two minutes) Sam would allow himself when sharing information on articles he'd read. This process worked well, and Sam, who often overshared in meetings as well, was able to work with his supervisor to translate this into more concise reports in team meetings.

If you are managing or working with an autistic individual who appears to be making social missteps at work, do not let the behaviors go unchecked. Chances are your colleague is missing or misreading a hidden curriculum issue. Many autistic individuals are aware they are susceptible to engaging in socially awkward or inappropriate behaviors or missing the social cues that others use to guide their actions in the workplace. These employees have worked hard to obtain the job and are equally motivated to retain it. Therefore, managers and colleagues can support employees on the spectrum in understanding the hidden curriculum by:

- Providing rules for social interactions – meetings, conferences, and social events
- Providing rules for daily activities – attire, schedules, and topics of conversation
- Using clear, concise language – no idioms, metaphors, or sarcasm

As with any feedback, this guidance should be delivered in a direct and respectful fashion. If you are giving feedback in response to a social misstep, never "call out" an individual in a public forum. Be mindful to talk to your autistic colleagues privately, providing them with the context of why the behavior they engaged in was inappropriate for the situation and how they could have handled it more effectively.

The Role of Executive Functioning

As discussed in Chapter 5, executive functioning skills are the cognitive processes that allow us to plan and manage our work and regulate our emotions. Challenges related to executive functioning are not limited to individuals on the autism spectrum. Many neurodivergent individuals, including those diagnosed with ADD, ADHD, non-verbal learning disabilities, dyslexia, depression, and traumatic brain injury, among other conditions, can struggle with executive functioning. It is important to understand that these challenges are not an indication of an individual's intelligence or skill sets but can affect how they perform their job.

Just as with the hidden curriculum, autistic employees who struggle with executive functioning will need managers and colleagues to work with them to guide them in learning how to manage certain aspects of their work. Difficulty understanding how one's tasks fit into a larger project, i.e., the context, is often coupled with executive functioning issues, so it is extremely important to help employees on the spectrum understand who is dependent on their assignments and how they will be used.

Robert joined a global financial services firm as an analyst. His role required him to gather data from multiple systems, managed by other units, to produce reports for his supervisor. Due to the operation of legacy systems, the formatting of the data was not consistent across those systems. Robert spent significant time detailing the errors in the data and the corrections needed to the systems, arguing with his manager about why the task he was assigned could not be done. Consequently, Robert was unable to deliver the reports during his early weeks on the job.

While the underlying issues Robert identified with the data and systems were correct, his executive functioning challenges were prohibiting him from seeing how he could still complete his assigned task by devising a solution to use the data as presented to meet his supervisor's needs. He also didn't understand how the reports he was tasked with preparing were to be used, so did not know what degree of flexibility he had in managing how the data was reported. Ultimately, Robert was assigned a new manager who now carefully explains the context of his assignments and works with him to ensure he understands the use of his work product, as well as the limitations of fixing the existing systems.

Just as with hidden curriculum issues, if you are managing or working with a colleague who appears to have executive functioning challenges, do not let them continue without intervention. Issues that may appear modest at the outset of a job can become larger challenges as tasks become more complex, so addressing them quickly is important. Most autistic individuals are aware of their struggles, if any, and will know if they have areas of executive functioning where they may need support.

If you have hired someone on the spectrum, and they are disclosed, ask them if there are any features of their working or learning style of which you should be aware. As a manager, you should ask this of all your new hires. Even if you do not have any guidance from the employee, the following suggestions can help support someone who appears to be struggling with executive functioning:

- When assigning work, confirm understanding by asking the employee to repeat back to you, in their own words, how they will go about the assignment. This can be done verbally or in writing.
- Provide timeframes and deadlines for assignments.
- Hold regular, and frequent, check-in meetings for longer-term projects.
- Assign work in shorter, more discrete tasks.
- Provide templates of similar assignments as a guidepost.

- Explain any dependencies/priorities if multiple tasks are assigned at the same time.

When engaging in the above strategies, remember that autistic or not, everyone receives and processes information differently. As discussed in Chapter 9, how we deliver information is as important as the information itself, so be sure you are using clear, concise language, free of idioms, metaphors, and sarcasm, and consider the three modalities of learning – visual, auditory, and kinesthetic – when working with autistic colleagues.

The Role of Anxiety

According to the Anxiety and Depression Association of America (ADAA), 56% of adults report that stress and anxiety impact their performance at work. More than half the time, that stress or anxiety is caused by deadlines or interpersonal relationships at work.[1] Autistic individuals, who may already have heightened levels of anxiety, may get caught in a vicious cycle of increasing anxiety as they try to manage work performance issues.

Just as it is important to minimize candidate anxiety during the interview process, as discussed in Chapter 10, it is equally important to consider the impact of anxiety on work performance and take measures to reduce work-related stress. One of the key actions you can take to prevent anxiety for autistic individuals is to preview new situations and upcoming assignments. Previewing (see Chapter 5) provides individuals with time to process new information and avoid the anxiety associated with sudden changes.

Another story we heard, from a parent who reached out to us to see if we could help her daughter remedy her employment situation, was that of Anika, a software tester. Anika's supervisor came by her desk to meet with her at the end of each day for 15 minutes to review her progress and discuss the next day's work. A few weeks into her employment, Anika's supervisor went on vacation for the week but did not tell Anika he would be away. Each day that week, as her supervisor did not stop by, Anika became increasingly agitated. On Friday, Anika saw the area vice president walking the floor, ran up to her and blurted out, "I know my boss hates me and wants to kill me!" Misunderstanding Anika's anxiety and outburst for a threat of violence, the area vice president had Anika fired and escorted out of the building.

The circumstances surrounding Anika's story could have been avoided with some simple previewing. For Anika, the change in routine, with no explanation, triggered severe anxiety. This anxiety was coupled with her inability to understand how she could handle her concern and how her behavior might be viewed by others. First, she could have asked a colleague if they'd seen the supervisor or what she could do in this situation. Second, she used language that could be seen as threatening, resulting in immediate termination. Had Anika's supervisor previewed with her that he was going to be away and provided her with a contact in his absence for any questions, she might still be employed. Unfortunately, we were not working with Anika's employer and could not intervene with them on her behalf after the fact. In addition to illustrating the value of previewing, this story also demonstrates the necessity of broad-based autism awareness training, discussed in Chapter 14.

Having autistic employees know that they can seek support for hidden curriculum and executive functioning challenges without fear of being stigmatized is crucial. This involves creating an inclusive environment that does not tolerate bullying. Studies by the National Autistic Society of the UK and the Autism Society in the US found that one-third and one in six autistic employees reported being bullied on the job, respectively.[2,3] Autistic individuals are no different than neurotypical employees in expecting and deserving respect and opportunities on the job. Even individuals who struggle to understand certain rules of social interactions will perceive when they are being mistreated.

Conclusion

Struggles in understanding the social rules of the workplace, challenges with executive functioning, and anxiety may impact how an autistic employee performs on the job. None of these factors, however, reflect an individual's intelligence or skill sets. It is important to distinguish between performance issues related to autism versus those that may be related to ability. Communicating in a clear and concise fashion, providing rules for social interactions, and previewing upcoming events and assignments can help colleagues on the spectrum perform at their best.

Notes

* The names of the individuals in these examples have been changed.
1 ADAA. "Highlights: Workplace Stress & Anxiety Disorders Survey." *Anxiety and Depression Association of America*, 2006. https://adaa.org/workplace-stress-anxiety-disorders-survey.
2 Bancroft, Katherine, Amanda Batten, Sarah Lambert, and Tom Madders. *The Way We Are: Autism in 2012*. London: The National Autistic Society, 2012. https://cnnespanol.cnn.com/wp-content/uploads/2017/04/50th-survey-report-2012.pdf.
3 Autism Society. "Bullying Prevention." January 29, 2021. https://www.autism-society.org/living-with-autism/how-the-autism-society-can-help/safe-and-sound/bullying-prevention/.

Epilogue

Temple Grandin, a scientist and activist on the autism spectrum, has been quoted as saying, "The most interesting people you'll find are ones that don't fit into your average cardboard box. They'll make what they need, they'll make their own boxes".[1] Neurodivergent individuals don't necessarily "fit in" to today's recruiting and interviewing practices, yet they are a growing and valuable part of the available talent pool for employers.

We hope this book has provided you with an understanding of the diversity of information processing, learning, and thinking styles that exist, and the value in creating processes that allow you to harness all types of "thinkers" in your organization. As a society, we are neurodiverse, with neurotypical and neurodivergent people living side-by-side. When approaching employment, our goal should be a workforce that reflects this neurodiversity and uses practices for finding and keeping talent that benefit all.

The movement to increase the inclusion of neurodivergent, and more specifically autistic, individuals in the workforce, while approaching a decade, is in many ways still in its infancy. In writing this book, our goal is to encourage employers to create hiring practices that will screen in, rather than exclude, people who think differently, and that it will eventually be considered the best approach for engaging with *all* talent.

Today, employers may feel the need to create special programs for hiring neurodivergent employees and work with third-party specialists to do so. Our hope for the future is that books and programs targeted at increasing neurodiversity in the workplace will no longer be necessary as hiring *all* kinds of minds becomes the norm.

Note

1 The Art of Autism. "105 Favorite Quotes about Autism and Aspergers." March 10, 2021. https://the-art-of-autism.com/favorite-quotes-about-autism-and-as pergers/.

Appendix

Example 7.1 – Job Description

DATA SCIENTIST- SHIPPING

At Shopify, we empower 600,000+ entrepreneurs all over the world. We're looking for hard-working, passionate people to help us make commerce better for everyone using data. One incredibly important area of focus for Shopify is Shipping. Shipping is usually one of the top marginal costs of running an online store.

We are looking for a Data Scientist who will work closely with the Shipping product team to drive optimization in this area through the development of machine learning models. Improving the shipping rate strategy for merchants and their customers will be one of many projects you will be working on.

Requirements:
- Experience implementing models at scale (including Machine Learning models)
- Experience using Python (including scikit-learn) or similar languages
- Experience analyzing data using SQL
- Experience using Spark
  Experience with statistical methods like regression, GLMs, or experiment design and analysis
  Exposure to Tableau, QlikView, Mode, Matplotlib, or similar data visualization tools

Option to work remotely available

Example 7.2 – Job Description

QA ENGINEER - INTERN

HireVue is looking to add an intern to their team of quality assurance engineers. If you are interested in software quality and testing an interesting product with a great company then keep reading!

The Job

As a QA engineer intern for one of the development teams you will

- Work directly with local and remote QA engineers
- Review product specifications for testability
- Develop and run test plans for new and updated functionality
- Diagnose issues and record accurate steps to reproduce them
- Run regression tests and record results

What You'll be Testing

You will be testing multiple parts of HireVue's cutting edge video intelligence platform. This includes video playback and recording, real-time video conferencing, coding challenges, and artificial intelligence. Your work will be augmenting customers' human decision-making process and helping them find higher quality talent faster.

HireVue's Current Stack

- Test Automation: Python, Selenium
- Backend: Python, Django, Celery, Go
- Frontend: React Mobile, ReactNative

Requirements

Successful applicants will have:

- Familiarity with a programming language
- Strong written communication skills

Optional skills:

- School or work experience with an issue tracking system like Jira or Clubhouse
- School or work experience with a test management system like TestRail

The Details

Where: South Jordan, UT

Hours: 20 hours per week

Duration: 12 weeks

About HireVue

HireVue is transforming the way companies discover, hire, and develop the best talent through Hiring Intelligence and its HireVue Video Interviewing platform. For more information, visit www.hirevue.com.

HireVue is committed to equal treatment and opportunity in all aspects of recruitment, selection, and employment without regard to gender, race, religion, national origin, ethnicity, disability, gender identity/expression, sexual orientation, veteran or military status, or any other category protected under the law. HireVue is an equal opportunity employer; committed to a community of inclusion, and an environment free from discrimination, harassment, and retaliation.

Example 7.3 – Job Description (Before)

Add short "About Company XYZ" statement.
A description of the role of the financial reporting team would be helpful.
Position: Regional Finance – Financial Reporting *Add title of the position.*
This is a challenging role supporting the financial reporting team within finance.
Core Responsibilities:
- Support the preparation of the financial statements for the various board of directors, executive committee, and audit committees.
- Maintain relationships and communication with internal audit and regulators to ensure proper coordination and liaison, validation and control, and timely and accurate responses are provided. *Assuming this will be done under the supervision of more senior staff: change to "Support senior staff in maintaining relationships and communicating with ..."*
- Communicate and interact with other areas across the organization, including business finance, GTO, compliance, and regional management to resolve issues pertaining to financial reporting. *Same as previous: "Support senior staff in communicating and interacting with ..."*
- Support, research, and prepare monthly average asset figures for regulatory reporting.
- Participate in various ad-hoc projects related to accounting changes and/or process efficiencies.
Skills/Requirements:
- Interpersonal skills with the ability to build collaborative relationships with various members within finance and internal and external stakeholders. *"Interpersonal skills" is vague: identify specific skills that are involved when working with these internal and external stakeholders.*
- The ability to work independently and with a small group of people, and to influence and engage across the organization. *Remove "to influence" as it is vague and may cause some candidates to self-select out.*
- Demonstrated desire to add significant value within a fast-paced environment. *Remove bullet as "add significant value" is vague and some autistic candidates will choose not to apply based on the representation of it being a "fast-paced environment".*
Academic/Knowledge Requirements:
Excel proficient *List some specific capabilities in Excel the candidate should have.*
College degree *Add preferred degree areas or financial training and/or experience.*
Add Company's Diversity and Inclusion statement.

Example 7.4 – Job Description (After)

STAFF ACCOUNTANT
About XYZ Bank
We are a leading bank …[Company's About statement here]
This role is within the regional finance division of the Corporate & Investment Bank (CIB) which includes XYZ Bank's corporate finance, global markets and global transaction banking businesses. The regional finance division is responsible for managing CIB's forward-looking business planning and strategic transformation initiatives. This includes doing all accounting, generating financial statements, reporting on key performance indicators, and making financial decisions in terms of capitalization and operations.
Position: Regional Finance – Financial Reporting – Staff Accountant
This is a challenging role supporting the financial reporting team within finance.
Core Responsibilities:
- Support the preparation of the financial statements for the various board of directors, executive committee, and audit committees.
- Support senior staff in maintaining relationships and communication with internal audit and regulators to ensure proper coordination and liaison, validation and control, and timely and accurate responses are provided.
- Support senior staff in communicating and interacting with other areas across the organization, including business finance, GTO, compliance, and regional management to resolve issues pertaining to financial reporting.
- Support, research, and prepare monthly average asset figures for regulatory reporting.
- Participate in various ad-hoc projects related to accounting changes and/or process efficiencies.
Skills/Requirements:
- Ability to effectively communicate with various members within finance and internal and external stakeholders, either in writing or verbally
- Ability to problem solve, with some guidance
- Ability to maintain a professional demeanor when interacting with others
- Ability to work independently and with a small group of people and to engage across the organization
Academic/Knowledge Requirements:
- Excel proficient, including experience with pivot tables and macros
- College degree in accounting or finance or completion of 2 levels of the CPA exam
XYZ Bank is an equal opportunity employer. We seek candidates without regard to age, race, color, ancestry, national origin, citizenship status, military or veteran status, religion, creed, disability, sex, sexual orientation, marital status, medical conditions as defined by applicable law, genetic information, gender, gender identity, gender expression, pregnancy, childbirth and related medical conditions, or any other characteristics protected by applicable federal, state, or local laws and ordinances.

Example 11.1 – Rephrased Interview Questions

Common Interview Questions	Rephrased Interview Questions
Tell me about yourself. (For some autistic candidates, they will not know where to start, what to include, and how much detail to give – from birth, where they grew up, and where they now live.)	Education: • Why did you pick the college you went to? • How did you decide on a major in …? • What course at college was your favorite and what did you like about it? What course did you find most difficult and how was it challenging? • What did you find was the most difficult thing to adjust to going to college from high school? Work/Volunteer Experience: • How did you identify the opportunity at XYZ company? What was your search methodology? • What were your responsibilities at XYZ company/ volunteer position? • What did you enjoy the most when you worked/ volunteered at XYZ company? • Why did you stop working/volunteering at XYZ company? Other: • Did you participate in any extracurricular activities at school? If so, how many hours a week were you allocating to these activities? • What do you enjoy doing in your free time?
Describe your dream job.	When reading a job description, what requirements do you look for to decide the job is a good one for you to apply for?
What are your greatest strengths?	When working on a school or work project, what are the tasks or aspects of the assignments at which you excel or enjoy the most?
What are your greatest weaknesses?	When working on a school or work project, what are the tasks or aspects of the assignments that you find are the hardest for you? What compensatory strategies do you have, or are working on, to improve in these areas?
What would your supervisor say are your strengths?	Based on feedback you've received, what do you think your supervisor would say are your strengths?
What would your supervisor say are your weaknesses or areas for improvement?	Based on feedback you've received, what do you think your supervisor would say are areas where you could use further development?
Describe a time you had to work on a team to accomplish a common goal. Please describe the situation, your actions, and the outcome.	Tell me about a time you worked on a project with a group of people to accomplish a common goal. Please describe the project, your responsibilities within the project team, and the results of the overall project.
Describe a difficult work or project situation and how you handled it.	Tell me about a time at work or school when you were working with others and the project was not going well. What was your role in the team and what did you do to help resolve the problems that occurred?
Where do you see yourself in five years?	Have you thought about career goals beyond this position? If so, what are your longer-term career goals?
Why should I hire you?	What skills do you think you have that make you the right candidate for this job?

Example 13.1 – Mentor–Mentee Guidelines

Mentor	Mentee
Areas of focus: • Office-related issues • Professional development • Performance management • Peer-to-peer interactions • Manager interactions • Navigating the office environment – socially and professionally	**Areas of focus:** • Office-related issues • Professional development • Performance management • Peer-to-peer interactions • Manager interactions • Navigating the office environment – socially and professionally
Engagement: • Learn about your mentee beforehand: review resume, LinkedIn profile, get permission from mentee to talk to their manager/HR for background information. • Get to know your mentee: feel confident asking questions and gently probing for information on where they struggle and where they believe they need guidance.	**Engagement:** • Know your mentor: research them (review their LinkedIn profile) before meeting • Know yourself: come prepared to talk about your strengths, challenges, and concerns
Meeting structure: • Define parameters for meeting and communicating upfront, i.e., how often will you meet? Do you prefer to communicate between meetings by email, text, or phone? • Set a minimum number of times to meet monthly, as well as a maximum amount of time to meet/interact each month. • Set an agenda for each meeting with a goal for the meeting.	**Meeting structure:** • Understand parameters for meeting and communicating upfront, i.e., how often will you meet? Does your mentor prefer to communicate between meetings by email, text, or phone? • Know how frequently you will meet with your mentor and understand the time limits they have established with you for meetings and discussions. • Come prepared to each meeting to actively share and discuss issues you have agreed to with your mentor, or issues that have arisen and you wish to raise with your mentor.
Follow up: • Schedule next meeting. • Recap in writing if there are any tasks the mentee has to follow up on.	**Follow up:** • Know when next meeting is scheduled. • Recap in writing if there are any tasks you need to follow up on and report back to your mentor on any tasks you need to complete prior to the next meeting.

Mentor–Mentee Suggested Agenda Topics

- Asking for help
- Understanding the company culture
- Understanding the performance review feedback process
- Asking for feedback on performance
- Reacting and responding to feedback (criticism) on performance
- Requesting more/less work
- Disagreeing with a co-worker or manager
- Sharing views in team meetings
- Managing difficult relationships
- Determining who I should take an issue to (escalating an issue)
- Requesting time off (vacation time vs. sick time vs. Paid Time Off)
- Overtime (how much is too much?)
- Experiencing anxiety (or emotional dysregulation) – what to do
- Accommodation request process
- Protocols around lunchtime and taking breaks
- Non-work related activities during working hours (i.e., a doctor's appointment, taking a personal phone call, checking personal emails)
- Participating in activities outside of work with work colleagues
- Attending work-related social functions (i.e., holiday parties)
- Using the internet at work

Glossary

Anxiety   Intense, excessive, and persistent worry and fear about everyday situations.

Autism spectrum disorder (ASD)   A developmental disorder characterized by difficulty with communication and social interactions. Other characteristics of ASD include sensory sensitivities, highly focused interests, and repetitive behaviors. Autism is a spectrum and includes individuals with exceptional intellectual capabilities as well as those with intellectual disabilities.

Central coherence   The ability to pull information from multiple sources into a unified whole or "big picture".

Cognitive styles   The habitual ways we process information for tasks involving decision-making, problem-solving, perception, and attention.

Context   The lens through which one views a situation or circumstance.

Deliberative mindset   A belief that it is necessary to gather all available information before making decisions, leading to more unbiased processing of information, increased critical thinking, and improved judgments.

Education versus training   Education is the process of teaching individuals broad-based knowledge about a subject, while training is a more targeted effort in providing individuals with the acquisition of specific knowledge or applied skill sets.

Employee assistance program   An employee benefit program that assists employees with personal problems and/or work-related problems that may impact their job performance, health, and mental and emotional well-being.

Employee retention rate   A statistic representing the ability of an organization to retain the individuals hired.

Executive functioning skills   The capabilities that allow us to put our knowledge and intelligence to work, such as organization, time management, initiating, prioritizing, transitioning, working memory, and regulating our emotions.

External mentor   Someone outside of an employee's organization who may act as an advocate for the employee, as well as serve as the mentee's confidant and provide critical feedback.

Fixed mindset   A belief that talents are innate and will not change; therefore, individuals with a fixed mindset will tend to avoid challenges and dislike negative feedback.

Generalization   The ability to transfer learning from one situation to another by recognizing similarities.

Growth mindset   A belief that talents can be developed through hard work, good strategies, and input from others.

Hidden curriculum   The unspoken or unwritten rules of behavior that allow us to "fit in" to any social situation in which we find ourselves.

Identity-first language   A reference that highlights a person's disability as key to their identity, e.g., autistic person.

Inference   A conclusion or "educated guess" that is not explicitly stated but is drawn from current evidence and past experience.

Internal mentor   Someone from within a person's organization, but not a direct supervisor or close colleague, who serves to provide guidance on the organizational culture, career development, and rules of social engagement.

Intuition   Something one knows from instinct rather than conscious consideration.

Invisible disability   Physical, mental, or neurological conditions that are not apparent but may cause limitations in an individual's social interactions, movements, senses, or daily life activities. Also referred to as hidden disabilities or non-apparent disabilities.

Job coach   A professional who has been trained to come into the workplace with the employee to support them in being successful on the job. Tasks of a job coach can range from teaching and supporting an employee with their assigned tasks, to helping them navigate the organizational rules, both written and unwritten.

Literal thinkers   Individuals who take the written and spoken word at face value and do not automatically understand what was implied. Also referred to as black-and-white thinkers.

Mindset   A mental attitude or inclination.

Neurodevelopmental disorders   Life-long, cognitively-based conditions, including autism, that affect social interactions, and whose challenges may vary according to life stage and circumstances.

Neurodivergent   An individual who thinks differently from the majority of individuals.

Neurodiverse   Refers to the variety of types of thinking among all individuals, meant to remove the stigma associated with terms used to define those who think differently from the majority of society.

Neurotypical   An individual who does not display any atypical ways of thinking.

Nothing about us without us   A slogan used to convey the idea that no policy or program should be established about or for a group of individuals without representation and participation from members of the affected group.

Onboarding   An ongoing process that occurs during the first months an individual is employed so that they develop a deeper understanding of the function of their department in the organization, their role within the department, how to perform their tasks, and how to navigate the organization to best perform in their role. Also referred to as organizational socialization.

Organizational socialization   See "Onboarding".

Orientation   A one-time event, usually completed within a day, that familiarizes new employees with features of your organization, such as the mission, values, lines of business, benefits plans, and company rules.

Person-first language   A reference that emphasizes the person over the disability, e.g., a person with autism.

Previewing   In the context of recruiting candidates, previewing provides an applicant with detailed information about what will happen prior to, during, and after the interview process.

Processing differences   Differences in receiving and responding to information that comes through the senses, in particular, how long it takes someone to process verbal, visual, or motor information. Processing speed is not an indication of intelligence.

Sensory overload   Occurs when one or more of the five senses are overstimulated by the environment, providing more information than the brain can receive and process.

Social cognitive abilities   One's abilities to understand and interact with others and in social situations.

Soft skills   The skills that allow individuals to interact effectively and harmoniously with other people, such as communication and listening. Individuals with strong soft skills are also referred to as having high social intelligence or emotional intelligence.

Theory of mind   The ability to understand what others are thinking without being told.

Unconscious bias   A stereotype or attitude towards certain groups or individuals that affects how one thinks of or interacts with those groups/individuals. Also referred to as implicit bias.

Universal design   Universal design is the process of creating products and environments that are accessible to all people, regardless of age, disability, or other factors.

Vocal prosody   The rhythm, stress, and intonation of speech that provide one with a significant amount of information beyond the actual words of the speaker.

Wrap-around transition programs   Programs for youth transitioning into adulthood who may need extra support learning independent living skills, completing post-secondary education, obtaining and retaining employment, and developing adult relationships.

References

ADA. "ADA Tool Kit: Website Accessibility Under Title II of the ADA." n.d. Accessed August 30, 2020. https://www.ada.gov/pcatoolkit/chap5toolkit.htm.

Adobe. "Adobe Supplier Diversity." n.d. Accessed March 30, 2020. https://www.adobe.com/diversity/strategy/industry/suppliers.html.

AMC. "Sensory Friendly Films." n.d. Accessed August 30, 2020. https://www.amctheatres.com/programs/sensory-friendly-films.

American Association for the Advancement of Science (AAAS). "Entry Point!" American Association for the Advancement of Science, n.d. Accessed September 19, 2020. https://www.aaas.org/programs/entry-point.

American Association of People with Disabilities (AAPD). "Update on 2020 AAPD Summer Internship Program." American Association of People with Disabilities, n.d. Accessed September 19, 2020. https://www.aapd.com/press-releases/update-2020-summer-intern-program/.

American Psychological Association (APA). "Prosody in Speech and Song." American Psychological Association, September 11, 2014. https://www.apa.org/pubs/highlights/peeps/issue-29#.

Annabi, Hala, E. W. Crooks, Neil Barnett, J. Guadagno, James R. Mahoney, J. Michelle, A. Pacilio, Hiren Shukla, and Jose Velasco. *Autism @ Work Playbook: Finding Talent and Creating Meaningful Employment Opportunities for People with Autism*. Seattle, WA: ACCESS-IT, The Information School, University of Washington, 2019.

Anxiety and Depression Association of America (ADAA). "Highlights: Workplace Stress & Anxiety Disorders Survey." Anxiety and Depression Association of America, 2006. https://adaa.org/workplace-stress-anxiety-disorders-survey.

Armstrong, Thomas. "Neurodiversity: A Concept Whose Time Has Come." Institute4Learning, n.d. Accessed February 14, 2021. https://www.institute4learning.com/resources/articles/neurodiversity/.

Armstrong, Thomas. "The Myth of the Normal Brain: Embracing Neurodiversity." *AMA Journal of Ethics* 17 (April 23, 2015): 348–352. https://doi.org/10.1001/journalofethics.2015.17.4.msoc1-1504.

Ashkenas, Ron. "How to Be an Effective Executive Sponsor." *Harvard Business Review*, May 18, 2015. https://hbr.org/2015/05/how-to-be-an-effective-executive-sponsor.

Ashwin, Chris, and Mark Brosnan. "The Dual Process Theory of Autism." In Morsanyi, Kinga and Ruth M. J. Byrne, eds. *Thinking, Reasoning, and Decision Making in Autism*. London: Routledge, 2020.

Austin, Robert D., and Gary P. Pisano. "Neurodiversity as a Competitive Advantage." *Harvard Business Review*, May 1, 2017. https://hbr.org/2017/05/neurodiversity-a s-a-competitive-advantage.

Autism Society. "Bullying Prevention." n.d. Accessed January 29, 2021. https://www .autism-society.org/living-with-autism/how-the-autism-society-can-help/safe-and -sound/bullying-prevention/.

Bancroft, Katherine, Amanda Batten, Sarah Lambert, and Tom Madders. "The Way We Are: Autism in 2012." London: The National Autistic Society, 2012. https:/ /cnnespanol.cnn.com/wp-content/uploads/2017/04/50th-survey-report-2012.pdf.

Baron-Cohen, Simon. "Theories of the Autistic Mind." *The Psychologist* 21, no. 2 (2008): 112–116.

Baron-Cohen, Simon. *The Pattern Seekers: How Autism Drives Human Invention*. New York: Basic Books, 2020.

Bauer, Talya N. "Onboarding New Employees: Maximizing Success." SHRM Foundation, 2010. https://www.shrm.org/foundation/ourwork/initiatives/res ources-from-past-initiatives/Documents/Onboarding%20New%20Employees .pdf.

Bernick, Michael. "Effective Autism (Neurodiversity) Employment: A Legal Perspective." *Forbes*, n.d. Accessed September 1, 2020. https://www.forbes.com /sites/michaelbernick/2019/01/15/effective-autism-neurodiversity-employment-a- legal-perspective/.

Bernick, Michael S. "Putting Autism to Work." *ChiefExecutive.Net* (blog), February 13, 2020. https://chiefexecutive.net/creating-a-targeted-neurodiversity-employme nt-initiative/.

Bernick, Michael. "The State of Autism Employment in 2021." *Forbes*, January 12, 2021. https://www.forbes.com/sites/michaelbernick/2021/01/12/the-state-of-au tism-employment-in-2021/.

Biko, Nikoletta. "Job Offer Acceptance Rate Metrics: Recruiting Metrics FAQ." Workable, September 15, 2017. https://resources.workable.com/tutorial/faq-job -offer-metrics.

BIMA. "The Voices of Our Industry: BIMA Tech Inclusion & Diversity Report 2019." BIMA, 2019. https://bima.co.uk/wp-content/uploads/2020/01/BIMA -Tech-Inclusion-and-Diversity-Report-2019.pdf.

Blume, Harvey. "Neurodiversity: On the Neurological Underpinnings of Geekdom." *The Atlantic*, September 30, 1998. https://www.theatlantic.com/magazine/arc hive/1998/09/neurodiversity/305909/.

Blustein, David L. "The Role of Work in Psychological Health and Well-Being: A Conceptual, Historical, and Public Policy Perspective." *American Psychologist* 63, no. 4 (2008): 228–240. doi:10.1037/0003-066x.63.4.228.

Bodner, Kimberly E., Christopher R. Engelhardt, Nancy J. Minshew, and Diane L. Williams. "Making Inferences: Comprehension of Physical Causality, Intentionality, and Emotions in Discourse by High-Functioning Older Children, Adolescents, and Adults with Autism." *Journal of Autism and Developmental Disorders* 45, no. 9 (September 2015): 2721–2733. https://doi.org/10.1007/s 10803-015-2436-3.

Boss, Jeff. "5 Questions That Identify Growth-Minded Employees." *Entrepreneur*, May 22, 2015. https://www.entrepreneur.com/article/246494.

Brown, Lydia. "Identity-First Language." Autistic Self Advocacy Network. n.d. Accessed July 11, 2021. https://autisticadvocacy.org/about-asan/identity-first-language/.

Bulluss, Erin, and Abby Sesterka. "Talking about Autism: Why Language Matters." *Psychology Today*, October 1, 2019. https://www.psychologytoday.com/blog/insights-about-autism/201910/talking-about-autism.

Burchi, Elisabetta, and Eric Hollander. "Anxiety in Autism Spectrum Disorder." AADA, March 26, 2018. https://adaa.org/learn-from-us/from-the-experts/blog-posts/consumer/anxiety-autism-spectrum-disorder.

Bureau of Labor Statistics. "Civilian Labor Force Level." FRED, Federal Reserve Bank of St. Louis, August 6, 2020. https://fred.stlouisfed.org/series/CLF16OV.

Capital One. "Diversity, Inclusion & Belonging." n.d. Accessed August 31, 2020. https://www.capitalone.com/diversity/business-resource-groups/.

Carson, Biz. "Google's Infamous Brain-Teaser Interview Questions Don't Predict Performance." *Business Insider*, October 6, 2015. https://www.businessinsider.com/google-brain-teaser-interview-questions-dont-work-2015-10.

Casey, Caroline. "Do Your D&I Efforts Include People with Disabilities?" *Harvard Business Review*, March 19, 2020. https://hbr.org/2020/03/do-your-di-efforts-include-people-with-disabilities.

Centers for Disease Control and Prevention (CDC). "Disability Impacts All of Us Infographic." Centers for Disease Control and Prevention, March 8, 2019. https://www.cdc.gov/ncbddd/disabilityandhealth/infographic-disability-impacts-all.html.

CDC. "Data and Statistics on Autism Spectrum Disorder." Centers for Disease Control and Prevention, March 25, 2020. https://www.cdc.gov/ncbddd/autism/data.html.

CDC. "CDC Releases First Estimates of the Number of Adults Living with ASD." Centers for Disease Control and Prevention, April 27, 2020a. https://www.cdc.gov/ncbddd/autism/features/adults-living-with-autism-spectrum-disorder.html.

CDC. "Key Findings: CDC Releases First Estimates of the Number of Adults Living with Autism Spectrum Disorder in the United States." Centers for Disease Control and Prevention, April 27, 2020b. https://www.cdc.gov/ncbddd/autism/features/adults-living-with-autism-spectrum-disorder.html.

CDC. "Diagnostic Criteria for Autism Spectrum Disorder (ASD)." Centers for Disease Control and Prevention, June 29, 2020. https://www.cdc.gov/ncbddd/autism/hcp-dsm.html.

Center on Budget and Policy Priorities. "Chart Book: SNAP Helps Struggling Families Put Food on the Table." n.d. Accessed November 7, 2019. https://www.cbpp.org/research/food-assistance/chart-book-snap-helps-struggling-families-put-food-on-the-table.

Cohen, Liz. "5 Reasons Growth Mindset Candidates Get the Job." Next Step Careers, n.d. Accessed March 10, 2021. http://ns-careers.com/blog/growthmindset.

College Autism Spectrum. "College Programs." n.d. Accessed September 19, 2020. http://collegeautismspectrum.com/collegeprograms/.

College Consultants. "Programs in College for Autism, Asperger, ADHD, LD, Neurodiversity." March 2, 2019. https://www.topcollegeconsultants.com/autism-in-college/.

Cone Communications. "Feeling Purpose: 2019 Porter Novelli/Cone Purpose Biometrics Study." 2019. https://www.conecomm.com/research-blog/purpose-biometrics.

Cox, Bradley, Amanda Mintz, Taylor Locks, Kerry Thompson, Amelia Anderson, Lindee Morgan, Jeffrey Edelstein, and Abigail Wolz. "Academic Experiences for College Students with Autism: Identity, Disclosure, and Accommodations." 2015. http://myweb.fsu.edu/bcox2/_pdf/AERA2015paper.pdf.

De Neve, Jan-Emmanuel, and George Ward. "Does Work Make You Happy? Evidence from the World Happiness Report." *Harvard Business Review*, March 20, 2017. https://hbr.org/2017/03/does-work-make-you-happy-evidence-from-the-world-happiness-report.

Deweert, Sarah. "Attention to Detail May Aid Visual Learning in Autism." *Spectrum Autism Research News* (blog), September 23, 2014. https://www.spectrumnews.org/opinion/attention-to-detail-may-aid-visual-learning-in-autism/.

Deweert, Sarah. "Repetitive Behaviors and 'Stimming' in Autism, Explained." *Spectrum Autism Research News* (blog), January 31, 2020. https://www.spectrumnews.org/news/repetitive-behaviors-and-stimming-in-autism-explained/.

Disabled World. "Invisible Disabilities: List and General Information." November 8, 2019. https://www.disabled-world.com/disability/types/invisible/.

Division of Labor Force Statistics. "Persons with a Disability, 2019. Current Population Survey (CPS)." US Bureau of Labor Statistics, February 26, 2020. https://www.dol.gov/sites/dolgov/files/odep/pdf/dol-odep-2019-briefing-appended-submission.pdf.

Dupont. "Supplier Diversity." n.d. Accessed February 1, 2021. https://www.dupont.com/supplier-center/supplier-diversity.html.

Dweck, Carol S. "What Having a 'Growth Mindset' Actually Means." *Harvard Business Review*, January 13, 2016a. https://hbr.org/2016/01/what-having-a-growth-mindset-actually-means.

Dweck, Carol S. *Mindset: The New Psychology of Success*. New York: Ballantine Books, 2016b.

Edelson, Stephen M. "Learning Styles & Autism." Autism Research Institute (blog), n.d. Accessed October 7, 2020. https://www.autism.org/learning-styles-autism/.

Ekman, Paul. *Emotions Revealed: Recognizing Faces and Feelings to Improve Communication and Emotional Life*. New York: Henry Holt, 2007.

Eng, Dinah. "Where Autistic Workers Thrive." *Fortune*, June 24, 2018. https://fortune.com/2018/06/24/where-autistic-workers-thrive/.

Fisher, Julia Freeland. "How to Get a Job Often Comes Down to One Elite Personal Asset, and Many People Still Don't Realize It." CNBC, December 27, 2019. https://www.cnbc.com/2019/12/27/how-to-get-a-job-often-comes-down-to-one-elite-personal-asset.html.

Gartner. "Gartner HR Survey Shows 86% of Organizations Are Conducting Virtual Interviews to Hire Candidates During Coronavirus Pandemic." Gartner, April 20, 2020. https://www.gartner.com/en/newsroom/press-releases/2020-04-30-gartner-hr-survey-shows-86--of-organizations-are-cond.

US Government Accountability Office (GAO). "Vocational Rehabilitation: Additional Federal Information Could Help States Serve Employers and Find Jobs for People with Disabilities." GAO-18-577. Washington, DC, September 6, 2018. https://www.gao.gov/assets/700/694369.pdf.

Ginac, Linda. "Impacts on Employee Engagement with Performance Management." HR Technologist, September 17, 2018. https://www.hrtechnologist.com/articles/employee-engagement/impacts-on-employee-engagement-with-performance-management/.

Glassdoor Economic Research. "The Rise of Mobile Devices in Job Search: Challenges and Opportunities for Employers." June 3, 2019. https://www.glassdoor.com/research/mobile-job-search/.

Grant, Stephanie, Frank Hodge, and Samantha Seto. "Can a Deliberative Mindset Prompt Reduce Investors' Reliance on Fake News?" SSRN Electronic Journal, February 19, 2021. https://ssrn.com/abstract=3444228.

Griffiths, Amy-Jane, Cristina M. Giannantonio, Amy E. Hurley-Hanson, and Donald N. Cardinal. "Autism in the Workplace: Assessing the Transition Needs of Young Adults with Autism Spectrum Disorder." Journal of Business and Management 22, no. 1 (2016): 5–22. https://www.chapman.edu/business/_files/journals-and-essays/jbm-editions/JBM-vol-22-no-1-Autism-in-the-Workplace.pdf.

Grund, Sandra. "What Every Job Seeker Should Know: Jobvite's 2020 Recruiter Nation Survey." Jobvite, October 13, 2020. https://www.jobvite.com/blog/hiring/what-every-job-seeker-should-know-jobvites-2020-recruiter-nation-survey/.

Haden, Jeff. "Why the Wrong Candidate Sometimes Gets Hired: Harvard Research Reveals People Prefer 'Naturals' Even When They Claim to Value Hard Work a Lot More." Inc., n.d. Accessed May 19, 2020. https://www.inc.com/jeff-haden/why-wrong-candidate-sometimes-gets-hired-harvard-research-reveals-people-prefer-naturals-even-when-they-claim-to-value-hard-work-a-lot-more.html.

Haigh, Sarah M., Jennifer A. Walsh, Carla A. Mazefsky, Nancy J. Minshew, and Shaun M. Eack. "Processing Speed Is Impaired in Adults with Autism Spectrum Disorder, and Relates to Social Communication Abilities." Journal of Autism and Developmental Disorders 48, no. 8 (August 1, 2018): 2653–2662. https://doi.org/10.1007/s10803-018-3515-z.

Hammett, Ellen. "What Brands Are Doing to Be More Inclusive for People with Disabilities." Marketing Week (blog), February 6, 2019. https://www.marketingweek.com/how-brands-are-being-more-inclusive-for-people-with-disabilities/.

Happé, Francesca, and Uta Frith. "The Weak Coherence Account: Detail-Focused Cognitive Style in Autism Spectrum Disorders." Journal of Autism and Developmental Disorders 36, no. 1 (2006): 5–25. https://doi.org/10.1007/s10803-005-0039-0.

Hawkins, Jon. "How to Write Disability-Friendly Content." Medium, May 18, 2020. https://medium.com/better-marketing/how-to-write-disability-friendly-content-277845b8c2ee.

Hedley, Darren, Mathilda Wilmot, Jennifer Spoor, and Cheryl Dissanayake. "Benefits of Employing People with Autism: The Dandelion Employment Program." DXC Dandelion Program 22 (2017). https://digitalcommons.ilr.cornell.edu/dandelionprogram/25.

Hurley-Hanson, Amy E., and Cristina M. Giannantonio. "Autism in the Workplace (Special Issue)." Journal of Business and Management 22, no. 1 (2016): 10. https://www.chapman.edu/business/_files/journals-and-essays/jbm-editions/JBM-vol-22-no-1-Autism-in-the-Workplace.pdf.

Idaho Department of Vocational Rehabilitation. "About VR." n.d. Accessed September 1, 2020. https://vr.idaho.gov/about/.

Internal Revenue Service. "Tax Benefits for Businesses Who Have Employees with Disabilities." n.d. Accessed March 22, 2020. https://www.irs.gov/businesses/smal l-businesses-self-employed/tax-benefits-for-businesses-who-have-employees-with -disabilities.

JDP. "New Study Reveals How Americans Prepare for Job Interviews in 2020." April 30, 2020. https://www.jdp.com/blog/how-to-prepare-for-interviews-2020/.

Kahneman, Daniel. *Thinking, Fast and Slow*. New York: Farrar, Straus and Giroux, 2013.

Kelly, Jack. "11 Complaints from Frustrated and Angry Job Seekers about the Interview Process." *Forbes*, n.d. Accessed August 31, 2020. https://www.forbes .com/sites/jackkelly/2019/08/12/11-complaints-from-frustrated-and-angry-job-s eekers-about-the-interview-process/.

Kruse, Kevin. "What Is Employee Engagement." *Forbes*, June 22, 2012. https://www .forbes.com/sites/kevinkruse/2012/06/22/employee-engagement-what-and-why/? sh=29bd188d7f37.

Kudisch, Jeffrey. "Turned Down for a Job? You Are Now One Rejection Closer to Success." *Los Angeles Times*, March 17, 2017. https://www.latimes.com/business /la-fi-career-coach-job-rejection-20170317-story.html.

Lai, Jonathan K. Y., Esther Rhee, and David Nicholas. "Suicidality in Autism Spectrum Disorder: A Commentary." *Advances In Neurodevelopmental Disorders* 1, no. 3 (2017): 190–195. doi:10.1007/s41252-017-0018-4.

Lebowitz, Shana, Allana Akhtar, and Marguerite Ward. "61 Cognitive Biases That Screw Up Everything We Do." *Business Insider*, May 5, 2020. https://www.bus inessinsider.com/cognitive-biases-2015-10.

Lime. "Leading Perspectives on Disability: A Q&A with Dr. Stephen Shore." March 22, 2018. https://www.limeconnect.com/opportunities_news/detail/leading-per spectives-on-disability-a-qa-with-dr-stephen-shore.

Linguist, Stacie L., and Kristin Jones Pierre. "OFCCP Revises Voluntary Self-Identification Disability Form." *The National Law Review*, May 11, 2020. https ://www.natlawreview.com/article/ofccp-revises-voluntary-self-identification-disa bility-form.

LinkedIn. "New Report: Women Apply to Fewer Jobs Than Men, But Are More Likely to Get Hired." n.d. Accessed August 31, 2020. https://business.linkedin .com/talent-solutions/blog/diversity/2019/how-women-find-jobs-gender-report.

Lloyd-Thomas, Peter. "Sensory Gating in Autism, Particularly Asperger's." *Epiphany* (blog), March 26, 2017. https://epiphanyasd.blogspot.com/2017/03/sensory-g ating-in-autism-particularly.html.

Mahan, Thomas F., Danny Nelms, Jeeun Yi, Alexander T. Jackson, Michael Hein, and Richard Moffett. "2020 Retention Report: Trends, Reasons & Wake Up Call." Work Institute, 2020. https://workinstitute.com/retention-report/.

Massachusetts General Hospital. "Why Do Those with Autism Avoid Eye Contact? Imaging Studies Reveal Overactivation of Subcortical Brain Structures in Response to Direct Gaze." ScienceDaily, n.d. Accessed October 7, 2020. www.sciencedaily .com/releases/2017/06/170615213252.htm.

Maurer, Roy. "How Many Open Reqs Should In-House Recruiters Have?" SHRM, August 6, 2018. https://www.shrm.org/resourcesandtools/hr-topics/talent-acqu isition/pages/how-many-open-reqs-should-in-house-recruiters-have.aspx.

McDermott, Catherine Tobin, and Brett Ranon Nachman "United States College Programs for Autistic Students." College Autism Network, January 25, 2021. https://collegeautismnetwork.org/wp-content/uploads/2021/01/College-Autism-Specific-Support-Programs-1.25.2021.pdf.

McKeever, Vicky. "How Much Eye Contact Is Too Much in a Job Interview?" CNBC, March 12, 2020. https://www.cnbc.com/2020/03/11/how-much-eye-contact-is-too-much-in-a-job-interview.html.

Medicaid. "How Much Do States Spend Per Medicaid Enrollee?" n.d. Accessed August 7, 2020. https://www.medicaid.gov/state-overviews/scorecard/how-much-states-spend-per-medicaid-enrollee/index.html.

Merhar, Christina. "Employee Retention: The Real Cost of Losing an Employee." PeopleKeep, June 2, 2020. https://www.peoplekeep.com/blog/employee-retention-the-real-cost-of-losing-an-employee.

Merriam-Webster Dictionary. s.v. "Mindset." n.d. Accessed February 8, 2021. https://www.merriam-webster.com/dictionary/mindset.

Merriam-Webster Dictionary. s.v. "Neurodiverse." n.d. Accessed February 8, 2021. https://www.merriam-webster.com/dictionary/neurodiverse.

Michigan State University. "Why Diversity Is Important in Supply Chain Management." MSU Online, September 28, 2018. https://www.michiganstateuniversityonline.com/resources/supply-chain/the-importance-of-diverse-suppliers/.

Microsoft. "AI for Accessibility – Microsoft AI." n.d.a. Accessed August 30, 2020. https://www.microsoft.com/en-us/ai/ai-for-accessibility.

Microsoft. "Autism Hiring Corporate." n.d.b. Accessed August 31, 2020. https://www.microsoft.com/en-us/diversity/inside-microsoft/cross-disability/autismhiringcorporate.

Moore, Emily. "The Most Common Reasons Candidates Reject Job Offers (& How You Can Prevent It!)." Glassdoor for Employers, July 26, 2018. https://www.glassdoor.com/employers/blog/common-reasons-reject-job-offers/.

Morsanyi, Kinga, and Ruth M. J. Byrne, eds. Thinking, Reasoning, and Decision Making in Autism. London: Routledge, 2020.

National Institute of Mental Health (NIMH). "Statistics: Any Anxiety Disorder." National Institute of Mental Health, November 2017. https://www.nimh.nih.gov/health/statistics/any-anxiety-disorder.shtml.

Office of Disability Employment Policy (ODEP). "Job Accommodation Network." Office of Disability Employment Policy, n.d. Accessed August 31, 2020. https://askjan.org/.

Okten, Irmak Olcaysoy. "Studying First Impressions: What to Consider?" APS Observer 31, no. 2 (January 31, 2018). https://www.psychologicalscience.org/observer/studying-first-impressions-what-to-consider.

Partnership on Employment & Accessible Technology. "Infographic: The Accessibility of Online Job Applications." Peatworks (blog), n.d. Accessed August 31, 2020. https://peatworks.org/digital-accessibility-toolkits/talentworks/make-your-erecruiting-tools-accessible/new-data-on-the-accessibility-of-online-job-applications/.

Partnership on Employment & Accessible Technology. "PEAT: Accessible Technology & The Employment Lifecycle." YouTube Video 2 (2017): 46. https://www.youtube.com/watch?v=45mkpIMkl-M.

Patankar, Vinay. "6 Checklists to Perfect Your New Employee Onboarding Process." *Process Street* (blog), February 2, 2018. https://www.process.st/new -employee-onboarding-process/.

PBS NewsHour. "3 Ways That the U.S. Population Will Change over the Next Decade." January 2, 2020. https://www.pbs.org/newshour/nation/3-ways-that-th e-u-s-population-will-change-over-the-next-decade.

Plain Language. "Federal Plain Language Guidelines." n.d. Accessed March 10, 2021. https://www.plainlanguage.gov/guidelines/.

Poem of Quotes. "I, Mudd Quotes." n.d. Accessed March 10, 2021. https://www .poemofquotes.com/quotes/film-tv/i-mudd-quotes.

PolicyWorks. "The Business Case for Hiring Workers with Disabilities." n.d. Accessed March 8, 2021. http://toolkit.disabilitypolicyworks.org/the-business-c ase-for-hiring-workers-with-disabilities/.

Qu, Linda. "99% of Fortune 500 Companies Use Applicant Tracking Systems (ATS)." *Jobscan Blog* (blog), November 7, 2019. https://www.jobscan.co/blog/99 -percent-fortune-500-ats/.

Renesi, Marianna. "Think Different: A Flashback of an Historical Campaign." *Medium*, March 25, 2018. https://medium.com/ad-discovery-and-creativity-lab/ think-different-b566c2e6117f.

Return on Disability Group. *2020 Annual Report Summary – The Global Economics of Disability.* n.d. Accessed March 22, 2021. http://rod-group.com/sites/default/ files/Summary%20Report%20-%20The%20Global%20Economics%20of%20 Disability%202020.pdf.

Return on Disability Group. *2016 Annual Report – The Global Economics of Disability*, May 2016. https://www.rod-group.com/content/rod-research/edit-res earch-2016-annual-report-global-economics-disability.

Robert Half. "62 Percent of Workers Would Relocate for a Job, Survey Finds." *Robert Half*, January 1, 2015. http://rh-us.mediaroom.com/2019-01-15-62-Perc ent-Of-Workers-Would-Relocate-For-A-Job-Survey-Finds.

Roberts, Paul. "The Art of Getting Things Done." *Fast Company*, May 31, 2000. https://www.fastcompany.com/39708/art-getting-things-done.

Rossi, Carey. "Autism Spectrum Disorder: Autistic Brains vs Non-Autistic Brains." *Psycom.Net* (blog), May 4, 2020. https://www.psycom.net/autism-brain-diff erences.

Roux, Anne M., Paul T. Shattuck, Jessica E. Rast, Julianna A. Rava, and Kristy A. Anderson. *National Autism Indicators Report: Transition into Young Adulthood.* Philadelphia, PA: Life Course Outcomes Research Program, A.J. Drexel Autism Institute, Drexel University, 2015.

Ryder, Leah. "How a T-Shirt Company Built an Inclusive, Visual Workplace with Trello." n.d. Accessed August 30, 2020. https://blog.trello.com/how-spectrum -designs-built-inclusive-visual-workplace-with-trello.

Scheiner, Marcia. "The Autistic Workforce Is Here. Are You Prepared?" *Training Industry* (blog), March 16, 2020. https://trainingindustry.com/articles/strategy-ali gnment-and-planning/the-autistic-workforce-is-here-are-you-prepared/.

Scheiner, Marcia, and Joan Bogden. *An Employer's Guide to Managing Professionals on the Autism Spectrum.* London: Jessica Kingsley, 2017.

Segal, R. P. "SAP Develops Workforce of the Future." n.d. Accessed October 6, 2020. https://www.triplepundit.com/story/2015/sap-develops-workforce-future/57881.

Shattuck, Paul T., Sarah Carter Narendorf, Benjamin Cooper, Paul R. Sterzing, Mary Wagner, and Julie Lounds Taylor. "Postsecondary Education and Employment among Youth with an Autism Spectrum Disorder." *Pediatrics* 129, no. 6 (June 2012): 1042. https://doi.org/10.1542/peds.2011-2864.

Sheikh, Knvul. "Noise Pollution Isn't Just Annoying: It's Bad for Your Health." Brainfacts.org, June 27, 2018. https://www.brainfacts.org:443/thinking-sensing -and-behaving/diet-and-lifestyle/2018/noise-pollution-isnt-just-annoying-its-bad -for-your-health-062718.

Silberman, Steve. *NeuroTribes: the Legacy of Autism and the Future of Neurodiversity.* New York: Avery, 2016.

Singh, Maanvi. "Young Adults with Autism More Likely to Be Unemployed, Isolated." NPR, n.d. Accessed August 7, 2020. https://www.npr.org/sections/h ealth-shots/2015/04/21/401243060/young-adults-with-autism-more-likely-to-be -unemployed-isolated.

Social Security Administration. "How You Qualify: Disability Benefits." n.d.a. Accessed August 7, 2020. https://www.ssa.gov/benefits/disability/qualify.html.

Social Security Administration. "SSI Federal Payment Amounts for 2020." n.d.b. Accessed August 7, 2020. https://www.ssa.gov/oact/cola/SSI.html.

Social Security Administration. "Understanding SSI – If You Are Disabled or Blind." n.d.c. Accessed August 7, 2020. https://www.ssa.gov/ssi/text-disable-ussi.htm #sgact.

Social Security Administration. "Disabled-Worker Statistics." June 2020. https://ww w.ssa.gov/oact/STATS/dib-g3.html.

Steinmetz, Erika. "U.S. Census Bureau Current Population Report: Americans with Disabilities: 2002." US Census Bureau, May 2006. https://www.census.gov/prod /2006pubs/p70-107.pdf.

Stuurman, S., H. J. M. Passier, Frédérieke Geven, and E. Barendsen. "Autism: Implications for Inclusive Education with Respect to Software Engineering." In CSERC '19: Proceedings of the 8th Computer Science Education Research Conference, Larnaca, Cyprus, 2019, 15–25. New York: Association for Computing Machinery (ACM). https://doi.org/10.1145/3375258.3375261.

Tang, Patrick. "A Brief History of Peer Support: Origins." *Peers for Progress*, June 7, 2013. http://peersforprogress.org/pfp_blog/a-brief-history-of-peer-support-origins/.

The Art of Autism. "105 Favorite Quotes about Autism and Aspergers." n.d. Accessed March 10, 2021. https://the-art-of-autism.com/favorite-quotes-about -autism-and-aspergers/.

The Recruiter Network. "How Recruiters Effectively Use Social Media." *The Recruiter Network Blog*, n.d. Accessed September 19, 2020. https://therecruiter network.com/blog/how-recruiters-effectively-use-social-media/.

Thompson, Derek. "The Science of Smart Hiring." *The Atlantic*, April 10, 2016. https://www.theatlantic.com/business/archive/2016/04/the-science-of-smart-h iring/477561/.

Tower, Jessica. "How to Hire for Growth Mindset with One Interview Question." March 27, 2017. http://jesstower.com/how-to-hire-for-growth-mindset-with-one -interview-question/.

Tulshyan, Ruchika. "How to Reduce Personal Bias When Hiring." *Harvard Business Review*, June 28, 2019. https://hbr.org/2019/06/how-to-reduce-personal-bias -when-hiring.

Turczynski, Bart. "2020 HR Statistics: Job Search, Hiring, Recruiting & Interviews." Zety, November 15, 2016. https://zety.com/blog/hr-statistics.

Turczynski, Bart. "2021 HR Statistics: Job Search, Hiring, Recruiting & Interviews." Zety, January 28, 2021. https://zety.com/blog/hr-statistics.

Twin Group. "8 Surprising Statistics about Interviews." Twin Employment & Training, March 2018. https://www.twinemployment.com/blog/8-surprising-statistics-about-interviews.

US Department of Labor. "About WIOA." n.d.a. Accessed September 1, 2020. https://www.dol.gov/agencies/eta/wioa/about.

US Department of Labor. "Section 503 Best Practices for Federal Contractors." n.d.b. Accessed August 7, 2020. https://www.dol.gov/agencies/ofccp/compliance-assistance/outreach/resources/section-503-vevraa/503.

US Equal Employment Opportunity Commission. "Your Employment Rights as an Individual with a Disability." n.d. Accessed May 19, 2020. https://www.eeoc.gov/facts/ada18.html.

Vermeulen, Peter. *Autism as Context Blindness*. Shawnee Mission, KS: AAPC Publishing, 2012.

Walker, Nick. "Neurodiversity: Some Basic Terms & Definitions." *Neurocosmopolitanism*, September 27, 2014. https://neurocosmopolitanism.com/neurodiversity-some-basic-terms-definitions/.

Watson, Kathryn. "Sensory Overload: Symptoms, Causes, Related Conditions, and More." *Healthline*, September 27, 2018. https://www.healthline.com/health/sensory-overload.

Weaver II, Elizabeth A., and Hilary H. Doyle. "How Does the Brain Work?" *Dana Foundation* (blog), August 11, 2019. https://www.dana.org/article/how-does-the-brain-work/.

Workable. "What Is Employee Retention?" Workable, August 29, 2019. https://resources.workable.com/hr-terms/what-is-employee-retention.

Workforce Recruitment Program (WRP). "Employers: Workforce Recruitment Program." n.d. Accessed September 19, 2020. https://www.wrp.gov/wrp?id=employer_landing_page.

World Economic Forum. "Want to Achieve Success? Develop a Strategic Mindset." July 6, 2020. https://www.weforum.org/agenda/2020/07/strategic-mindset-success/.

Zaboski, Brian A., and Eric A. Storch. "Comorbid Autism Spectrum Disorder and Anxiety Disorders: A Brief Review." *Future Neurology* 13, no. 1 (February 2018): 31–37. https://doi.org/10.2217/fnl-2017-0030.

Zwick, Dalia. "Posture and Gait in Individuals with Autism Spectrum Disorder (ASD)." n.d. Accessed November 12, 2020. https://www.yai.org/news-stories/blog/posture-and-gait-individuals-autism-spectrum-disorder-asd.

Index